PRIMARY

MATHEMATICS

3B

Home Instructor's

Guide

Authored by: Jennifer Hoerst
Printed by: Avyx, Inc.

Go to:
www.avyx.com

Or e-mail:
info@avyx.dom

Or write:
Avyx, Inc.
8032 South Grant Way
Littleton, CO 80122-2705
USA
303-483-0140

ISBN 13: 978-1-887840-79-8

Printed in the United States of America

Preface and General Instructions

This guide is meant to help instructors using *Primary Mathematics 3B* when teaching one student or a small group of students. It should be used as a guide and adapted as needed. It contains

 objectives,

 notes to the instructor, providing added explanation of concepts,

 instructional ideas and suggested activities,

 and ideas for games

to reinforce concepts from the

 corresponding textbook pages, learning tasks, and

 "homework" assignments.

Included is a <u>suggested</u> weekly schedule and pages for mental math (in the appendix). The schedule is simply to help you keep on track – you need to spend more time on a topic if necessary and less time if your student is proficient in the topic. Practices and reviews in the text are scheduled as they are encountered, and can be done independently by the student, or can be used as part of a lesson. Since some of the practice questions are challenging, they provide good opportunities for discussion. When there are several practices one after the other, you may want to go on to the next topic and insert the rest of the practices later to allow for more ongoing review. The mental math pages can be used as worksheets and many can also be done orally, with your student seeing the problem and answering out loud rather than writing the answer down. They can be used any time after they are referenced in this guide, and can be used more than once for more practice. So if four Mental Math pages are listed for one lesson, they are not meant to all be done during that lesson, but can be used any time after that lesson for review and mental math practice.

Answers to the workbook exercises are given at the end of this guide.

This guide can be used with both the third edition and the U.S. edition of *Primary Mathematics 2A*.

3d› indicates portions pertaining only to the third edition, and

US› indicates portions pertaining only to the US edition (except for number words).

U.S. spellings and conventions will be used in this guide. Answers involving number words will use the current U.S. convention of reserving the word "and" for the decimal and not using it in number words for whole numbers.

Contents

Suggested schedule ⋯⋯ i
Additional Materials ⋯⋯ v

Unit 1   Mental Calculation
  Part 1   **Addition** (pp. 6-7) ⋯⋯ 1
           (1) Tens and Ones ⋯⋯ 1
           (2) Make 10 ⋯⋯ 5
  Part 2   **Subtraction** (pp. 8-9) ⋯⋯ 7

           (1) Tens and Ones ⋯⋯ 7
           (2) Subtract from a Ten ⋯⋯ 11
           Enrichment 1 Mental Math ⋯⋯ 13
           Enrichment 2 Mental Math ⋯⋯ 14
  Part 3   **Multiplication** (p. 10) ⋯⋯ 15
           (1) Multiplication by Tens or Hundreds ⋯⋯ 15
  Part 4   **Division** (pp. 11-13) ⋯⋯ 17
           (1) Division of Tens, Hundreds, and Thousands ⋯⋯ 17
           Practice 1A ⋯⋯ 18
           Practice 1B ⋯⋯ 18

Unit 2   Length
  Part 1   **Meters and Centimeters** (pp. 14-18) ⋯⋯ 19
           (1) Meters and Centimeters ⋯⋯ 19
           (2) Addition and Subtraction of Compound Units ⋯⋯ 22
           Practice 2A ⋯⋯ 25
  Part 2   **Kilometers** (pp. 19-23) ⋯⋯ 26
           (1) Kilometers ⋯⋯ 26
           (2) Addition and Subtraction of Compound Units ⋯⋯ 29
           Practice 2B ⋯⋯ 31
  Part 3   **Yards, Feet, and Inches** (US▸pp. 24-26) ⋯⋯ 32
           (1) Yards, Feet, and Inches ⋯⋯ 32
           (2) Addition and Subtraction of Compound Units ⋯⋯ 36
  Part 4   **Miles** (US▸pp. 27-28) ⋯⋯ 38
           (1) Miles ⋯⋯ 38
           Practice 2C ⋯⋯ 39

Unit 3   Weight
  Part 1   **Kilograms and Grams** (US▸pp. 29-33 3d▸pp. 24-28) ⋯⋯ 40
           (1) Kilograms and Grams ⋯⋯ 40
           (2) Addition and Subtraction of Compound Units ⋯⋯ 42
           Practice 3A ⋯⋯ 43
  Part 2   **More Word Problems** (US▸pp. 34-38 3d▸pp. 29-33) ⋯⋯ 44
           (1) Word Problems ⋯⋯ 44
           Practice 3B ⋯⋯ 47
  Part 3   **Pounds and Ounces** (US▸pp. 39-42) ⋯⋯ 48
           (1) Pounds and Ounces ⋯⋯ 48
           Practice 3C ⋯⋯ 51

Review (US▸pp. 43-44 3d▸pp. 40-41) ⋯⋯ 52

Unit 4	**Capacity**	
Part 1	**Liters and Milliliters** (US▸pp. 45-52 3d▸pp. 36-43)	53
	(1) Kilograms and Grams	53
	(2) Converting between Liters and Milliliters	55
	(3) Addition and Subtraction of Compound Units	56
	Practice 4A	57
	Practice 4B	57
Part 2	**Gallons, Quarts, Pints, and Cups** (US▸pp. 53-56)	58
	(1) Gallons, Quarts, Pints, and Cups	58
	Practice 4C	61
	Review (US▸p. 57 3d▸pp. 44)	62
Unit 5	**Graphs**	
Part 1	**Bar Graphs** (US▸pp. 58-63 3d▸pp. 45-50)	63
	(1) Bar Graphs I	63
	(2) Bar Graphs II	65
Unit 6	**Fractions**	
Part 1	**Fractions of a Whole** (US▸pp. 64-69 3d▸pp. 51-56)	66
	(1) Fractions of a Whole	66
	(2) Comparing Fractions	68
	Practice 6A	70
Part 2	**Equivalent Fractions** (US▸pp. 70-75 3d▸pp. 57-62)	71
	(1) Equivalent Fractions by Multiplication	71
	(2) Equivalent Fractions by Division	74
	(3) Simplest Form	76
	(4) Comparing Fractions	77
	Practice 6B	81
	Review (US▸pp. 76-77 3d▸pp. 63-64)	82
Unit 7	**Time**	
Part 1	**Hours and Minutes** (US▸pp. 78-86 3d▸pp. 65-73)	83
	(1) Telling Time and Duration	83
	(2) Converting Between Hours and Minutes	85
	(3) Time Intervals	87
	(4) Adding and Subtracting Hours and Minutes	89
	Practice 7A	92
Part 2	**Other Units of Time** (US▸pp. 87-89 3d▸pp. 74-76)	93
	(1) Seconds	93
	(1) Years, Months, and Weeks	94
	Practice 6B	96
	Review (US▸pp. 90-91 3d▸pp. 77-78)	97
Unit 8	**Geometry**	
Part 1	**Angles** (US▸pp. 92-95 3d ▸pp. 79-82)	98
	(1) Angles	98
	(2) Right Angles	99
	Enrichment 3 – Möbius Strip	101

Unit 9   **Area and Perimeter**
  Part 1   **Area** (US▸pp. 96-100 3d▸pp. 83-87) ································ 102
                 (1) Square Units ··· 102
                 (2) Units of Area ·· 103
  Part 2   **Perimeter** (US▸pp. 101-104 3d▸pp.88-91) ······················· 105
                 (1) Perimeter ·· 105
  Part 3   **Area of a Rectangle** (US▸pp. 105-107 3d▸pp. 92-94) ·········· 107
                 (1) Area of a Rectangle ·· 107
                 Enrichment 3 – Pentominoes ·· 109

         Review (US▸pp. 108-112 3d▸pp. 95-96) ······························ 111

Answers to Workbook Exercises and Reviews
         Exercise 1 ··· 114
         Exercise 2 ··· 114
         Exercise 3 ··· 114
         Exercise 4 ··· 115
         Exercise 5 ··· 115
         Exercise 6 ··· 115
         Exercise 7 ··· 116
US▸ Exercise 8 ··· 116
3d▸ Exercise 8 ··· 117
3d▸ Exercise 9 ··· 117
3d▸ Exercise 10 ·· 117
US▸ Exercise 9, 3d▸ Exercise 11 ··· 118
US▸ Exercise 10 ·· 118
         Exercise 10a (appendix) ··· 118
US▸ Exercise 11 ·· 119
         Exercise 11a (appendix) ··· 119
         Exercise 12 ·· 120
US▸ Exercise 13 ·· 120
3d▸ Exercise 13 ·· 120
3d▸ Exercise 14 ·· 121
US▸ Exercise 14 3d▸ Exercise 15 ··· 121
US▸ Exercise 15 3d▸ Exercise 16 ··· 121
US▸ Exercise 16 ·· 121
         Exercise 16a (appendix) ··· 122
         Review 1 ·· 122
         Review 2 ·· 123
         Exercise 17 ·· 123
         Exercise 19 ·· 123
         Exercise 20 ·· 124
         Exercise 21 ·· 124
US▸ Exercise 22 ·· 124
3d▸ Exercise 22 ·· 125
3d▸ Exercise 23 ·· 125
US▸ Exercise 23 ·· 125
         Exercise 23a (appendix) ··· 126
         Exercise 24 ·· 126
         Exercise 25 ·· 126
         Review 3 ·· 126

Review 4 ······ 127
Exercise 26 ······ 127
Exercise 27 ······ 128
Exercise 28 ······ 128
Exercise 29 ······ 128
Exercise 30 ······ 129
Exercise 31 ······ 129
Exercise 32 ······ 129
Exercise 33 ······ 130
Exercise 34 ······ 130
Exercise 35 ······ 130
Review 5 ······ 131
Review 6 ······ 131
Exercise 36 ······ 132
Exercise 37 ······ 132
Exercise 38 ······ 133
Exercise 39 ······ 133
Exercise 40 ······ 133
Exercise 41 ······ 134
Exercise 42 ······ 134
Exercise 43 ······ 134
Exercise 44 ······ 134
Review 7 ······ 135
Exercise 45 ······ 135
Exercise 46 ······ 135
Exercise 47 ······ 135
Exercise 48 ······ 135
Exercise 49 ······ 136
Exercise 50 ······ 136
Exercise 51 ······ 136
Exercise 52 ······ 136
Review 8 ······ 136
Review 9 ······ 137

Answers to Mental Math ······ 138

Appendix A
Mental Math ······ a1
10x10 squares ······ a16
Fraction Circles ······ a17
Fraction Strips ······ a19
Centimeter Graph Paper ······ a19

Appendix B
Length Part 3 Yards, Feet, and Inches Learning Tasks ⋯⋯⋯⋯⋯⋯⋯⋯⋯ b1
Exercise 10a ⋯⋯⋯⋯⋯⋯⋯⋯⋯⋯⋯⋯⋯⋯⋯⋯⋯⋯⋯⋯⋯⋯⋯⋯⋯⋯⋯⋯ b2
Exercise 11a ⋯⋯⋯⋯⋯⋯⋯⋯⋯⋯⋯⋯⋯⋯⋯⋯⋯⋯⋯⋯⋯⋯⋯⋯⋯⋯⋯⋯ b3
Practice 2D ⋯⋯⋯⋯⋯⋯⋯⋯⋯⋯⋯⋯⋯⋯⋯⋯⋯⋯⋯⋯⋯⋯⋯⋯⋯⋯⋯⋯⋯ b6
Weight Part 3 Pounds and Ounces Learning Tasks ⋯⋯⋯⋯⋯⋯⋯⋯⋯⋯ b7
Exercise 16a ⋯⋯⋯⋯⋯⋯⋯⋯⋯⋯⋯⋯⋯⋯⋯⋯⋯⋯⋯⋯⋯⋯⋯⋯⋯⋯⋯⋯ b8
Practice 3D ⋯⋯⋯⋯⋯⋯⋯⋯⋯⋯⋯⋯⋯⋯⋯⋯⋯⋯⋯⋯⋯⋯⋯⋯⋯⋯⋯⋯⋯ b9
Capacity Part 2 Gallons, Quarts, Pints, and Cups Learning Tasks ⋯⋯⋯ b10
Exercise 23a ⋯⋯⋯⋯⋯⋯⋯⋯⋯⋯⋯⋯⋯⋯⋯⋯⋯⋯⋯⋯⋯⋯⋯⋯⋯⋯⋯⋯ b11
Practice 4D ⋯⋯⋯⋯⋯⋯⋯⋯⋯⋯⋯⋯⋯⋯⋯⋯⋯⋯⋯⋯⋯⋯⋯⋯⋯⋯⋯⋯⋯ b12

Suggested Weekly Schedule

Week	Part	Lesson	Textbook Pages	Exercises	Additional Material	Appendix
Unit 1: Mental Calculation						
1	1 Addition	(1) Tens and Ones	6-7	WB Ex. 1	Base-10 blocks	Mental Math 1
		(2) Make Tens	7	WB Ex. 2	Number discs	Mental Math 2
	2 Subtraction	(1) Tens and Ones	8-9		10x10 grid	Mental Math 3
		(2) Subtract from a Ten		WB Ex. 3	Playing cards	Mental Math 4
		Enrichment 1				Mental Math 5 Mental Math 6
		Enrichment 2				Mental Math 7 Mental Math 8
2	3 Multiplication	(1) Multiplication by Tens or Hundreds	10	WB Ex. 4	Base-10 blocks Number discs	Mental Math 9
	4 Division	(2) Division of Tens, Hundreds, and Thousands	11	WB Ex. 5	Number cards	Mental Math 10 Mental Math 11 Mental Math 12
		Practice	12-13	TB Practice 1A TB Practice 1B		
Unit 2: Length						
3	1 Meters and Centimeters	(1) Meters and Centimeters	14-16	WB Ex. 6	Ruler Meter stick Measuring tape Base-10 bocks Playing cards	
		(2) Addition and Subtraction of Compound Units	17	WB Ex. 7		
		Practice	18	TB Practice 2A		
	2 Kilometers	(1) Kilometers	19-21	US➤WB Ex. 8 3d➤WB Ex. 8 WB Ex. 9 WB Ex. 10		
		(2) Addition and Subtraction of Compound Units	22	US➤WB Ex. 9 3d➤WB Ex. 11		
		Practice	23	TB Practice 2B		
4	3 Yards, Feet and Inches	(1) Yards, Feet and Inches	US➤24-25	US➤WB Ex. 10	Ruler Yardstick Linking cubes	Appendix b1-b3
		(2) Addition and Subtraction of Compound Units	US➤26			
	4 Miles	(1) Miles	US➤27	US➤ WB Ex. 11		Appendix b4-b5
		Practice	US➤28	US➤ TB Practice 2C		Appendix b6
Unit 3: Weight						
5	1 Kilograms and Grams	(1) Kilograms and Grams	US➤29-31 3d➤ 24-26	US➤WB Ex. 12 WB Ex. 13 3d➤WB Ex. 12 WB Ex. 13 WB Ex. 14	Balance Metric weights Weighing scales	
		(2) Addition and Subtraction of Compound Units	US➤32 3d➤27	US➤WB Ex. 14 3d➤WB Ex. 15		

Week	Part	Lesson	Textbook Pages	Exercises	Additional Material	Appendix
		Practice	US➤33 3d➤28	TB Practice 3A		
	2 More Word Problems	(1) Word Problems	US➤34-37 3d➤29-32	US➤WB Ex. 15 3d➤WB Ex. 16		
		Practice	US➤38 3d➤33	TB Practice 3B		
6	3 Pounds and Ounces	(1) Pounds and Ounces	US➤39-41	US➤WB Ex. 16	Balance pound weight	Appendix b7-b8
		Practice	US➤42	US➤ TB Practice 3C		Appendix b9
	Review		US➤43-44 3d➤34-35	TB Review A TB Review B WB Review 1 WB Review 2		
	Unit 4: Capacity					
7	1 Liters and Milliliters	(1) Liters and Milliliters	US➤45-48 3d➤36-39	WB Ex. 17 WB Ex. 18 WB Ex. 19	Beakers or measuring cups with ml markings.	
		(2) Converting between Liters and Milliliters	US➤48-49 3d➤39-40	WB Ex. 20 WB Ex. 21		
		(3) Addition and Subtraction of Compound Units	US➤50 3d➤41	US➤WB Ex. 22 3d➤WB Ex. 22 WB Ex. 23		
		Practice	US➤51-52 3d➤42-43	TB Practice 4A TB Practice 4B		
8	2 Gallons, Quarts, Pints, and Cups	(1) Gallons, Quarts, Pints, and Cups	US➤53-55	US➤WB Ex. 23	Measuring cups Various containers Linking cubes Playing cards	Appendix b10-b11
		Practice	US➤56	US➤ TB Practice 4C		Mental Math 13 Practice 4C Practice 4D (appendix b12)
	Review		US➤57 3d➤44	TB Review C		
	Unit 5: Graphs					
9	1 Bar Graphs	(1) Bar Graphs I	US➤58-61 3d➤45-48	WB Ex. 24	Linking cubes	
		(2) Bar Graphs II	US➤62-63 3d➤49-50	WB Ex. 25		
	Review			WB Review 3 WB Review 4		
	Unit 6: Fractions					
10	1 Fractions of a Whole	(1) Fractions of a Whole	US➤64-66 3d➤51-53	WB Ex. 26 WB Ex. 28	Linking cubes Fraction cards	Fraction bars Fraction circles
		(2) Comparing Fractions	US➤67-68 3d➤54-55	WB Ex. 29 WB Ex. 30		
		Practice	US➤69 3d➤56	TB Practice 6A		
11	2 Equivalent Fractions	(1) Equivalent Fractions by Multiplication	US➤70-72 3d➤57-59	WB Ex. 31 WB Ex. 32	Paper strips Number cards	Fraction bars
		(2) Equivalent Fractions by Division	US➤73 3d➤60	WB Ex. 33		

Week	Part	Lesson	Textbook Pages	Exercises	Additional Material	Appendix
		(3) Simplest Form	US➤73-74 3d➤60-61	WB Ex. 34		
12		(4) Comparing Fractions	US➤74 3d➤61	WB Ex. 35		
		Practice	US➤75 3d➤62	TB Practice 6B		
	Review		US➤76-77 3d➤63-64	TB Review D WB Review 5 WB Review 6		
	Unit 7: Time					
13	1 Hours and Minutes	(1) Telling Time and Duration	US➤78-81 3d➤65-68	WB Ex. 36 WB Ex. 37	Analog clock Digital clock that shows seconds Stopwatch	Mental Math 14
		(2) Converting Between Minutes and Hours	US➤82 3d➤69	WB Ex. 38		
		(3) Time Intervals	US➤83 3d➤70	WB Ex. 39		
		(4) Adding and Subtracting Hours and Minutes	US➤84-85 3d➤71-72	WB Ex. 40		
		Practice	US➤86 3d➤73	TB Practice 7A		
14	2 Other Units of Time	(1) Seconds	US➤87 3d➤74	WB Ex. 41 WB Ex. 42		
		(2) Years, Months, and Weeks	US➤88 3d➤75	WB Ex. 43 WB Ex. 44		
		Practice	US➤89 3d➤76	TB Practice 7B		
	Review		US➤90-91 3d➤77-78	TB Review E WB Review 7		
	Unit 8: Geometry					
15	1 Angles	(1) Angles	US➤92-93 3d➤79-80	WB Ex. 45	Index cards Brad fastener	
	2 Right Angles	(1) Right Angles	US➤94-95 3d➤81-82	WB Ex. 46		
		Enrichment 3				
	1 Area	(1) Square Units	US➤96-97 3d➤83-84	WB Ex. 47		
		(2) Units of Area	US➤98-100 3d➤85-87	WB Ex. 48 WB Ex. 49	Square and half-squares	Graph paper Enrichment 3
16	2 Perimeter	(1) Perimeter	US➤98-100 3d➤88-91	WB Ex. 50	Linking cubes	Graph paper
	3 Area of a Rectangle	(1) Area	US➤105-106 3d➤92-93	WB Ex. 51 WB Ex. 52		Enrichment 4
		Practice	US➤107 3d➤94	TB Practice 9A		
		Enrichment 4				
17	Review		US➤108-112 3d➤95-96	TB Review F US➤ TB Review G WB Review 8 WB Review 9		

Additional Material

Base-10 set.

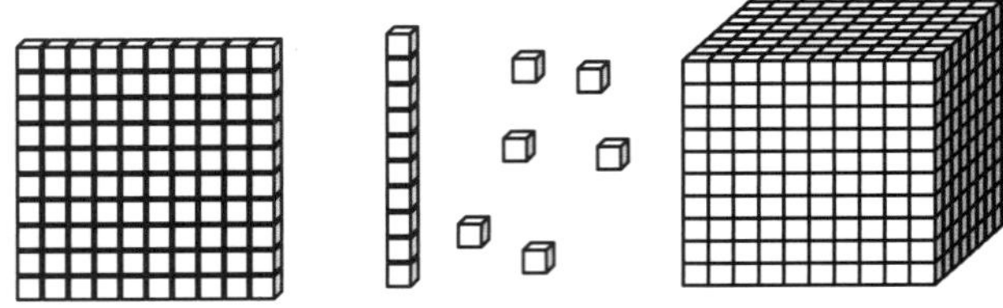

Number discs - Use plastic or cardboard discs and write "10,000" on one disc, "1000" on eighteen discs, "100" on eighteen discs, "10" on eighteen discs, and "1" on eighteen discs. If you have colored plastic counters, you can use one color for each place value.

Multilink cubes or other linking cubes or objects.

Place Value Chart
large enough to hold up to nine number discs each in the top and bottom halves.

Thousands	Hundreds	Tens	Ones

Hundred Chart
Make one or buy one with squares large enough to hold counters or coins.

1	2	3	4	5	6	7	8	9	10
11	12	13	14	15	16	17	18	19	20
21	22	23	24	25	26	27	28	29	30
31	32	33	34	35	36	37	38	39	40
41	42	43	44	45	46	47	48	49	50
51	52	53	54	55	56	57	58	59	60
61	62	63	64	65	66	67	68	69	70
71	72	73	74	75	76	77	78	79	80
81	82	83	84	85	86	87	88	89	90
91	92	93	94	95	96	97	98	99	100

Index cards for number cards and fact cards.
Playing cards, Dice
Ruler, meter stick, yard stick, tape measure
Balance and **metric weights**, a **pound weight** (e.g. fishing weight, food item)
Measuring cups: Liter or quart measuring cup which shows metric measure as well as customary measures, teaspoons, medicine spoon that shows milliliters.
Fraction strips (see appendix)
Clock: A real analog (face) clock with a second hand or a **Demonstration clock** with geared hands.
Digital clock or analog clock showing seconds.
Stopwatch
Calendar

Unit 1 Mental Calculation

Part 1 Addition

(1) Tens and Ones

 ➢ Add 2-digit numbers mentally by adding tens and then ones.

 In *Primary Mathematics 2A* and *Primary Mathematics 3A*, students learned to add using a vertical format and the formal algorithm in which the ones were added first, 10 ones renamed as a ten, and then the tens added. The student still needs to practice the formal algorithm and can use it when needed.

If this is the first time using Primary Mathematics, it may seem to you that the mental math strategies are just a complication to simply using the standard algorithm, so why bother trying to teach new strategies. It is up to you if you want to teach these strategies. However, using mental calculation strategies increases number sense. Some of the mental math strategies learned in earlier levels of *Primary Mathematics* will be reviewed here.

Mental math strategies learned in earlier levels of *Primary Mathematics* and new ones introduced here include the following. (Number bonds are shown here to illustrate these strategies, but students should not be required to draw these number bonds.)

➢ Add 1, 2, or 3 by counting on.

   $59 + 2 = 61$; count on 60, 61.

$$7 + 5 = 10 + 2 = 12$$
$$3 \quad 2$$

➢ Add two 1-digit numbers whose sum is greater than 10 by making a 10. (This strategy is useful for students who know the addition and subtraction facts through 10, but have trouble memorizing the addition and subtraction facts through 20.)

$$7 + 5 = 10 + 2 = 12$$
$$2 \quad 5$$

   $7 + 5 = 12$

➢ Add tens to 2 digit numbers by adding the tens.

$$48 + 20 = 68$$
$$8 \quad 40$$

   $48 + 20 = 68$

➢ Add a 1-digit number to a 2-digit number by adding the ones together.

$$47 + 2 = 40 + 9 = 49$$
$$40 \quad 7$$

   $47 + 2 = 49$

- ➢ Add a 1-digit number to a 2-digit number where adding the ones results in a number greater than 10 by
  - ○ making a 10

    $68 + 5 = 73$

  - ○ using basic addition facts.

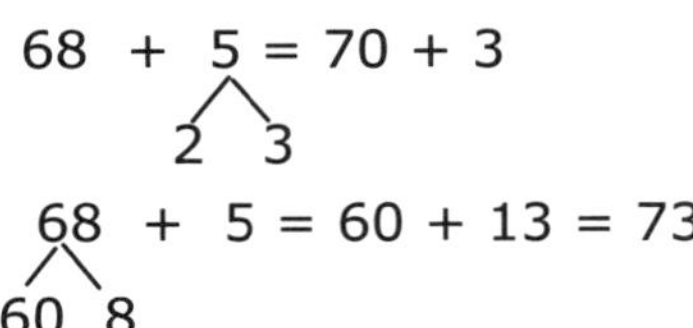

- ➢ Add a 2-digit number to a 2-digit number by adding the tens and then the ones, using the strategies already learned for adding tens and 1-digit numbers.

    $48 + 25 = 73$

- ➢ Add a 2-digit number to a 2-digit number by making a ten. (This strategy is new here.))

    $48 + 25 = 50 + 23 = 73$

- ➢ Add a 2-digit number to a 2-digit number by adding the next ten and then subtract an appropriate number of ones. (This strategy is new here.)

    $48 + 25 = 25 + 50 - 2 = 75 - 2 = 73$

- ➢ Add a number close to 100 by making 100.

    $57 + 98 = 155$

- ➢ Add a number close to 100 by first adding 100 and then subtracting the difference.

    $57 + 98 = 57 + 100 - 2 = 157 - 2 = 155$

Your student does not have to write the intermediate step unless the problem specifies an intermediate step. He can add the tens, and before writing the tens down he can "look ahead" to see if adding the ones will increase the sum of the tens by 1. By this time, he should know that 9 + 5 is greater than 10, He can write down the sum of the tens plus one more (8). Then he can determine the ones either by thinking of what remains in the ones when a ten is made (9 needs 1 to make a 10, take it from the 5, leaving 4) or recalling the addition fact 9 + 5 = 14 and writing down the 4.

 If your student is new to *Primary Mathematics* and did not use the earlier levels, you may wish to teach him the mental math strategy of making 10 when adding a 1-digit number to another 1-digit number or to a 2-digit number if the sum of the ones is more than 10. This is a useful strategy if your student has trouble recalling addition facts for sums between 10 and 20.

Draw a 10 by 2 array.

Write **7 + 5**. Your student may recall the addition fact 7 + 5 = 12.

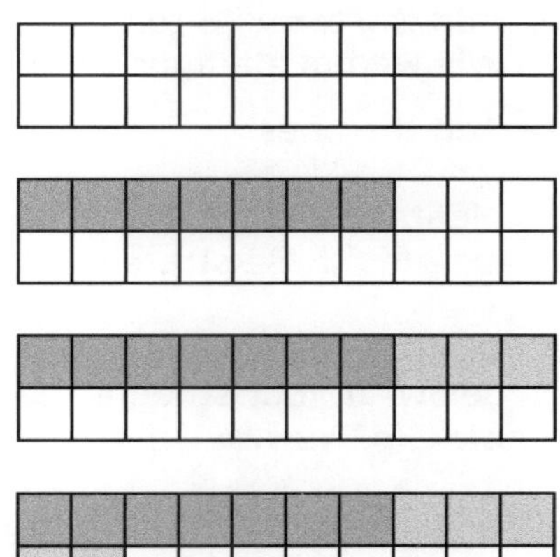

Color in 7 squares in the first row. Ask him how many more are needed to make a 10. (3 more are needed.)

Color in the other 3 squares a different color.

Ask him how many would be left if the 3 needed to make a 10 were taken from the 5 (2 are left). Color in 2 squares in the second row with the second color.

 If your student is new to *Primary Mathematics* and has not learned to add 2-digit numbers horizontally rather than vertically, have her practice adding any 1-digit number to a 2-digit number, tens to a 2-digit number, and a 2-digit number to a 2-digit number when there is no renaming (trading in ten ones for a ten).

Discussion:	Write:
	58 + 6
Does adding the ones give a number greater than ten? (Yes.) What would that make the tens in the answer? (6)	58 + 6 = **6**_
How many ones will there be? We can obtain the ones either by making a 10 (take 2 from the 6 to add to the 8, leaving 4) or by recalling the addition fact (8 + 6 = 14).	58 + 6 = 6**4**
Provide other examples for practice.	
	49 + 30
We can add these numbers by simply adding the tens. Which digit is the tens digit for the first number? (4) Which digit is the tens in the second number? (3) 4 tens and 3 tens are how many tens? (7)	49 + 30 = **7**_
How many ones there are? (9) Write down 9 for the ones.	49 + 30 = 7**9**
Provide other examples for practice.	
	34 + 62
Which digits are the tens? (3 and 6) What is the sum of the tens? (3 tens + 6 tens = 9 tens, or 30 + 60 = 90)	34 + 62 = **9**_
Which digits are the ones? (4 and 2) What is the sum of the ones? (4 ones + 2 ones = 6 ones, or 4 + 2 = 6)	34 + 62 = 9**6**
Provide other examples for practice.	

---

69 + 50

Add the tens. (6 tens + 5 tens = 11 tens)
Will we have a hundred in the answer? (Yes)

69 + 50 **= 11_**

Add the ones.

69 + 50 = 11**9**

Mental Math 1 in the appendix of this guide provides further practice, and extends these strategies to adding to a 3-digit number.

 Discuss strategies for adding 2-digit numbers. A suggested procedure is given below. If your student has trouble with any of the following, use **base-10 blocks, number discs,** or **dimes** and **pennies** to illustrate the steps.

Discussion:	Write:

---

45 + 33

How many tens are in the second number? (3)
Add the tens to the first number.

45 + 33 = **45 + 30 + 3**
         = **75 + 3**

Add the ones. (5 + 3 = 8)

45 + 33 = **78**

---

45 + 38

Add the tens of the second number to the first number.

45 + 38 = **45 + 30 + 8**
         = **75 + 8**

Add the ones. The tens will have to be increased by 1. We can add the ones by either making a 10 or recalling the fact 5 + 8 = 13.

45 + 38 = **83**

---

26 + 47

Add the tens and remember them. (6)
Look at the ones. Is the sum of the ones more than 10? (Yes) Add 1 to the tens. How many tens are there now? (6 + 1 = 7). Write down the tens.

26 + 47 = **7_**

We can obtain the ones by making a ten or recalling the math facts.

26 + 47 = 7**3**

 **Page 6 and Learning Tasks 1-3, p. 7**

1.   (a) 33; 37; 37   (b) 84; 90; 90   (c) 78; 83; 83
2.   (a) 71   (b) 114
3.   (a) 73   (b) 87   (c) 135   (d) 77   (e) 40
    (f) 72   (g) 59   (h) 62   (i) 81

 **Workbook Exercise 1**

(2) Make Ten

➢ Add 2-digit numbers mentally by making a 10 or a 100.

In *Primary Mathematics 2B*, the student learned strategies to mentally add a number close to 100, such as 95 or 98. These strategies will be reviewed here, and a new strategy involving making tens will be taught.

Review strategies for adding 95-99.

Discussion: Write:

To add these numbers, we can make a hundred. How much needs to be added to the 98 to make 100? (2) If we take that from the 18, how much is left? (16) We can add the 16 to the 100 we made with 98. What is the sum? (116)

$$98 + 18 =$$

$$98 + 18 = 116$$

2   16

100

116

Another way to add a number close to 100 is to add 100. If we add 100 instead of 97 to 46, how much too much have we added? (3) What do we have to do to get the correct sum? (Subtract 3)

$$46 + 97 =$$

$$46 + 97 = 46 + 100 - 3$$
$$= 146 - 3$$
$$= 143$$

You can use a **10x10 grid** (there is one in the appendix that may be copied), or **base-10 blocks** to illustrate addition of 2-digit numbers by making a 10. You can use a 100-flat and place 10-rods and unit cubes on top of it.

Discussion: Write:

Color in squares in the grid to show these two numbers. Look at the larger of the two numbers. What is the next 10? (50)
How much needs to be added to 47 to make it 50? (3) If you take 3 from the 24, what does this leave? (21).

We can add what is left to the fifty we made. We have taken 3 off of one number, and added 3 onto the other number, to get the sum of the two numbers.

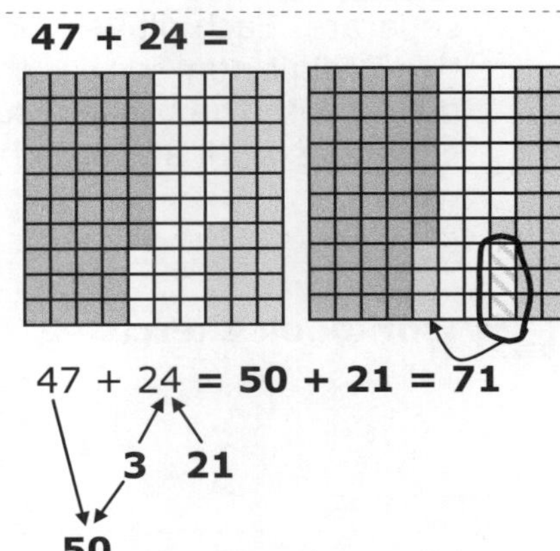

$$47 + 24 =$$

$$47 + 24 = 50 + 21 = 71$$

3   21

50

Is there another way we can add these numbers?
If we add 50 to 24, how much too much are we
adding? (3)
We can add 50, then take away the extra 3.

$$47 + 24 = 24 + 50 - 3$$
$$= 74 - 3$$
$$= 71$$

$$37 + 68 =$$

Think of a related problem where we are adding a
ten. (37 + 70). Find the sum.

$$37 + 70 = 107$$

How much more is this sum than 37 + 68? (2
more). If we take away 2 from this sum, we will
have the sum of 37 and 68.

$$37 + 68 = 105$$

$$\uparrow 2 \text{ less} \uparrow$$

$$37 + 70 = 107$$

or

$$37 + 68 = 105$$
$$2$$

$$35 + 70 = 105$$

 **Learning Tasks 4-5, p. 7**

4.   74

5.   (a) 66   (b) 92   (c) 110

 **War**

Material: Two decks of playing cards with the face cards and tens removed.
Separate the red and black cards into two separate decks.

Procedure: Shuffle and deal out all the red and black cards, keeping them
separate. Each player turns over two cards from each of their decks and forms
two 2-digit numbers, with the red cards as tens, and adds the numbers. The
player with the highest sum gets all the cards that have been turned over. Play
continues until all cards have been turned over. The player with the most cards
wins.

 **Workbook Exercise 2**

Part 2 Subtraction

(1) Tens and Ones

 ➢ Subtract 2-digit numbers mentally by subtracting tens and then ones.

 In *Primary Mathematics 2A* and *Primary Mathematics 3A*, students learned to subtract using a vertical format and the formal algorithm. The student still needs to practice the formal algorithm and can use it when needed.

Mental math strategies learned in earlier levels of *Primary Mathematics* and new ones introduced here include the following.

➢ Subtract 1, 2, or 3 by counting back.
  51 – 2 = 49; count back 50, 49.
  302 – 3 = 299; count back 301, 300, 299

$$48 - 20 = 28$$
$$8 \quad 40 - 20 = 20$$
$$28$$

➢ Subtract tens from a 2-digit numbers by subtracting the tens.

  48 – 20 = 28

$$47 - 2 = 45$$
$$40 \quad 7 - 2 = 5$$
$$45$$

➢ Subtract a 1-digit number from a 2-digit number when there are enough ones by subtracting the ones.

  47 – 2 = 45

$$65 - 8 = 52$$
$$5 \quad 60 - 8 = 52$$
$$57$$

➢ Subtract a 1-digit number from a 2-digit number when there are not enough ones by

  o subtracting from a 10

  o using basic subtraction facts

  65 – 8 = 57

$$65 - 8 = 57$$
$$50 \quad 15 - 8 = 7$$
$$57$$

➢ Subtract a 2-digit number from a 2-digit number by subtracting the tens and then the ones, using the strategies already learned for subtracting tens and 1-digit numbers.

  75 – 38 = 37

$$75 \xrightarrow{\ -\ 30\ } 45 \xrightarrow{\ -\ 8\ } 37$$

➤ Subtract a 2-digit number from a 2-digit number by subtracting from the nearest ten. (This strategy is new here.)

75 – 38 = 37

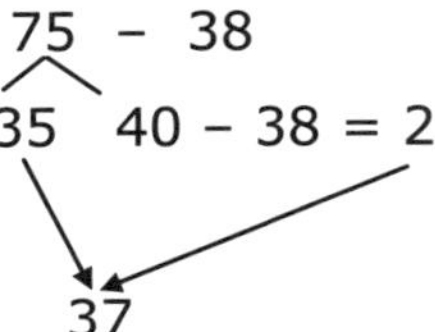

➤ Subtract a 2-digit number from a 2-digit number by subtracting the next ten and then adding back in an appropriate number of ones. (This strategy is new here.)

75 – 38 = 75 – 40 + 2 = 35 + 2 = 37

➤ Subtract a number close to 100 by subtracting 100 and then adding back the difference.

457 – 98 = 457 – 100 + 2 = 357 + 2 = 359

If your student hs not used earlier levels of *Primary Mathematics*, spend some time with the concept of subtracting from the ten. Although your students may be comfortable with subtracting by recalling the subtraction facts, and able to use that in mental calculations, the idea of subtracting from the next higher place value has applications in the sections on subtracting measurements in compound units.

 If your student is new to *Primary Mathematics* and did not use the earlier levels, you may want to teach her the mental math strategy of subtracting from a ten when there are not enough ones. A suggested procedure is given here. Use **dimes** and **pennies** for illustration.

Discussion:	Write:

Get a dime and 3 pennies.
How much money is this? (13 cents)
We want to buy something that costs 7 cents.   **13 – 7**

What would we give the cashier, the dime or the pennies? Since there are not enough pennies, we would give the dime.
What change would we get? (3 cents)   13 – 7 = **3 + 3 = 6**
How much money do we now have? (6 cents)
To get the amount we now have, we had to add the change to the pennies we started with.

Now get 4 dimes and 3 pennies.
We want to buy something that costs 7 cents.
What would we give the cashier? (One of the dimes) How much change would we get?
(3 cents)

How much money do we now have? (36)
We have one less dime, and the number of
pennies is the sum of the change from a dime
and the pennies we started out with.

$$43 - 7 = 30 + 3 + 3 = 36$$

We can subtract ones where there are not enough ones to subtract from by
subtracting from a ten. Go through a few other written examples. If your
student is not used to this strategy, and can recall the subtraction facts to 20
easily, she may not want to use it. Do not require that she use this method;
she only needs to be aware of it.

➤ If your student has not used *Primary Mathematics* before now and is not used
to doing this kind of problem horizontally, show her that she can use her facts
and still do it mentally. For example, in 75 – 9, she can "look ahead" to see
that she will have to rename one of the tens to get 15 ones in order to subtract
the 9. She can write down the 6 for the tens, and then write down the answer
to the subtraction fact

15 – 9. 75 – 9 = 66

Give her other examples to practice with. Mental Math 3 has some problems
that can be used for practice

➤ If your student is new to *Primary Mathematics* and has not learned to subtract
2-digit numbers horizontally rather than vertically, show her how to do this
when there is no regrouping.

Discussion: Write:

58 - 32

To subtract numbers, we can sometimes start with the highest
place value rather than the lowest. What digits are the tens in
both numbers? (5 and 3). Find their difference. (2)
We are subtracting the tens, so this is the tens of the answer.   58 - 32 = **2_**
What digits are the ones in both numbers? (8 and 2). Find
their difference. (6) This is the ones of the answer.   58 – 32 = 2**6**

We don't have to rewrite problems vertically if we pay
attention to which digits are the tens and which are the ones,
and we subtract tens from tens and ones from ones.

➤ Provide other examples to practice with. Mental Math 3 can be used for
practice.

 Discuss strategies for subtracting 2-digit numbers. A suggested procedure is given below. If your student has trouble with any of the following, use **base-10 blocks, number discs,** or **dimes** and **pennies** to illustrate the steps.

Discussion:	Write:
	63 - 20
Look at the tens and find the difference.	63 - 20 = **43**
	63 – 28
Subtract the tens of the second number from the first.	63 – 28 = **63 – 20 – 8** = **43 – 8**
Are there enough ones to subtract the 8? (No) We need to regroup a ten or subtract from a ten. There will be one less ten in the answer. Find the ones of the answer. Try subtracting from the ten. 10 – 8 = 2, 2 + 3 = 5	63 – 28 = **3_**
Or, use the subtraction fact 13 – 8 = 5	63 – 28 = 3**5**
	84 – 46
We can look ahead before subtracting the tens to see if we will have to subtract the ones from a ten or rename a ten. If we do, we can write down one less ten. What is the difference between the tens? (4) Will we end up with one less ten? (Yes)	84 – 46 = **3_**
Now find the ones.	84 – 46 = 3**8**

Provide other examples if necessary.

 **Page 8 and Learning Tasks 1-5, pp. 8-9**

1.   (a) 55; 53; 53   (b) 36; 30; 30   (c) 43; 35; 35

2.   (a) 49   (b) 46

3.   (a) 40   (b) 25
     (c) 8   (d) 52
     (e) 80   (f) 38

4.   (a) 16   (b) 30
     (c) 26   (d) 32
     (e) 40   (f) 8

(2) Subtract from a Ten

 ➢ Subtract 2-digit numbers mentally by subtracting from a ten or a hundred.

 In *Primary Mathematics 2B* the student learned some strategies for subtracting a number close to 100, such as 97. This will be reviewed here for students who have not done *Primary Mathematics 2B*, and a similar strategy for subtracting a number near any ten will be taught.

 If necessary, illustrate the strategies for subtracting from a ten with **base-10 blocks, number discs, or money**.

Discussion: Write:

We can subtract a number close to 100 by subtracting from the 100. If we subtract 98 from 100, what does that leave? (2)
Add that to the 36.
We can also do this problem by counting back 100, then forward 2.

136 - 98 =

$$136 - 98 = 36 + 2 = 38$$

$$136 \quad 98$$
$$36 \quad 100$$
$$2$$
$$38$$

What is the ten closest to 27? (30)
We can split 80 into 50 and 30 and mentally subtract 27 from 30.

What is 30 – 27? (3)
Then we add the 3 to the 50.
What is 80 – 27? (53)

If we subtract 30 from 80, how many too many are we taking away? (3)
So how many do we add back in to get the right answer? (3)

Provide other examples if necessary.

80 – 27 =

$$80 – 27$$
$$50 \quad 30$$

$$80 – 27 = \mathbf{50 + 3 = 53}$$
$$50 \quad 30$$
$$3$$
$$\mathbf{53}$$

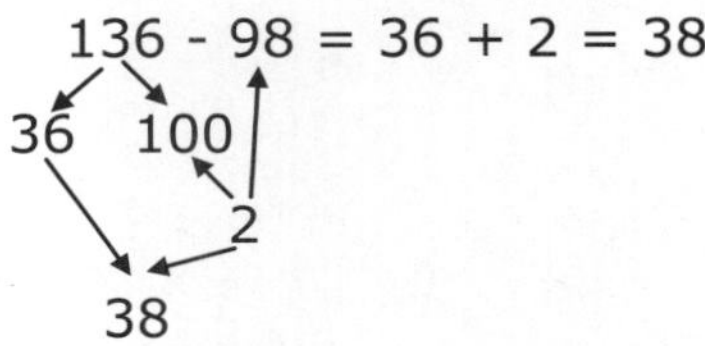 **Learning Tasks 5-6, p. 9**

5.   72

6.   (a) 2   (b) 4   (c) 5   (d) 33
     (e) 11   (f) 22   (g) 24   (h) 12   (i) 51

 **War**

<u>Material</u>: A deck of playing cards with the face cards and tens removed.

<u>Procedure</u>: Shuffle and deal out all cards. Each player turns over three cards. The highest card is a ten. The player forms a 2-digit number out of the other two cards and subtracts it from the 10. For example, a 5, 8, and 2 are turned over. The 8 is used as 80. The player uses the 5 and 2 to make 52 and subtract it from 80 to get 28. The player with the lowest difference gets all the cards that have been turned over. Play continues until all cards have been turned over. The player with the most cards wins.

 **Workbook Exercise 3**

Enrichment 1
Mental Math
Addition and Subtraction of 3-Digit Numbers

The strategies for mental math learned in the first unit of *Primary Mathematics 3* can be applied to larger numbers. These types of operations can be done without rewriting the problem vertically and applying the standard algorithms. Students may develop their own strategies. One strategy is given here.

$$267 + 80 = 347$$

Before writing the sum of the hundreds ($2 + 0 = 2$) down, "look ahead" to see if adding the tens will increase the hundreds by 1. They will, so the hundreds digit of the answer is 3. Then add the digits in the tens place, either by making a ten (8 needs two more to make a 10, take that from 6, leaving 4) or recalling the math facts ($8 + 6 = 14$). The next digit is 4. The ones digit is 7.

$$312 - 50 = 262$$

Before writing down the difference for the hundreds ($3 - 0 = 3$), "look ahead" to see if subtracting the tens requires regrouping one of the hundreds. It does, so write down a 2 instead of a 3. Then find the tens using the tens digit, either by subtracting from 10 (subtract 5 from 10, leaving 5, which is added to 1 to give 6) or recalling the math facts ($11 - 5 = 6$). The tens digit is 6. The ones digit of the answer is 2.

$$466 + 86 = 552$$

Add the hundreds. (4) Before writing down the hundreds, look ahead. Adding the tens will increase the hundreds by 1. Write down 5. Add the tens. This gives a tens digit of 4. Look ahead. Adding the ones increases the tens by one, so write down 5. Add the ones. The ones digit is 2.

$$452 - 86 = 366$$

Subtract the hundreds. (4) Before writing down the hundreds, look ahead. Subtracting the tens will decrease the hundreds by one since there are not enough tens from which to subtract. So write down 3. Subtract the tens ($15 - 8 = 7$). Before writing down 7, look ahead. Subtracting the ones will decrease the tens by one since there are not enough ones from which to subtract 6. So write down 6 instead of 7. Subtract the ones. ($12 - 6 = 6$) Write down the ones.

Discuss strategies for adding and subtracting 2-digit numbers. You can use the problems from the Mental Math pages in the appendix.

Mental Math 5 has problems involving renaming only once. Mental Math 6 is more challenging and has problems involving renaming twice.

Enrichment 2
Mental Math
Number Pairs that Make 100 or 1,000

Subtraction from 100 or 1000 and recognition of number pairs that make 100 or 1000 is a useful mental math strategy that will help in strategies for adding and subtracting in compound units, such as addition and subtraction of meters and centimeters or kilograms and grams. These strategies were covered in earlier levels of Primary Math.

In a number pair whose sum is a multiple of 10, the sum of the digits in the same place value is nine, except for the digit in the lowest place value, where the sum is 10.

For example:

	Hundreds	Tens	Ones
37 + 63 = 100		3 + 6 = 9	7 + 3 = **10**
98 + 2 = 100		9 + 0 = 9	8 + 2 = **10**
70 + 30 = 100		7 + 3 = 10	No ones
234 + 766 = 1000	2 + 7 = 9	3 + 6 = 9	4 + 6 = **10**
912 + 88 = 1000	9 + 0 = 9	1 + 8 = 9	2 + 8 = **10**
520 + 480 = 1000	5 + 4 = 9	8 + 2 = **10**	No ones
600 + 400 = 1000	6 + 4 = **10**	No tens	No ones

When subtracting from 100 or 1000, think of the number that makes a 9 with each digit except the last; for that one think of the number that makes a 10 with it.

	Hundreds	Tens	Ones	Answer
100 – 45		9 – 4 = 5	10 – 5 = 5	55
1000 – 754	9 – 7 = 2	9 – 5 = 4	10 – 4 = 6	246
1000 – 333	9 – 3 = 6	9 – 3 = 6	10 – 3 = 7	667
1000 – 340 Since there are no ones, the tens have to make 10.	9 – 3 = 6	10 – 4 = 6		660
1000 – 3 Think of the second number as 003.	9 – 0 = 9	9 – 0 = 9	10 – 3 = 7	997
1000 – 23 Think of the second number as 023.	9 – 0 = 9	9 – 2 = 7	10 – 3 = 7	977
1000 – 40 There are no ones, so the tens have to make a 10.	9 – 0 = 9	10 – 4 = 6		960

Review these strategies and examples with your student. More practice is available in Mental Math 7 in the appendix of this guide.

Part 3 Multiplication

(1) Multiplication by Tens or Hundreds

 ➢ Multiply tens or hundreds by a 1-digit number.

 In Primary Mathematics 3A the student learned how to multiply tens and hundreds by a one digit number. This is reviewed here.

➤ Use **base-10 blocks**, if necessary, to illustrate the following.

Discussion: Write:

                                         4 x 2
What is the product?   4 x 2 = **8**

                                         4 ones x 2 = 8 ones

What is 40 x 2?   **40 x 2**

We can cover up the 0 with   **4 tens x 2 = 8 tens**
a finger, or imagine it cut   **40   x 2 = 80**
off, multiply 4 by 2, and
then stick the 0 back on.

What is 400 x 2?   **400 x 2 =**
We can cover up the two 0's   **4 hundreds x 2 = 8 hundreds**
in 800, find the product of 4   **400   x 2 = 800**
and 2, then add the 0's back
on.

For each of these, we can   **5   x 3 = 15**
multiply the non-zero digit,   **50   x 3 = 150**
5, by the 3, write the   **500 x 3 = 1500**
answer, and then add the
same number of 0's on to
the answer as comes after
the 5.

Why are there three 0's after the 4 of the last answer   **5   x 8 = 40**
instead of two 0's when there are only two 0's after the 5?   **50   x 8 = 400**
The extra 0 comes from the answer to 5 x 8, or 40. 40   **500 x 8 = 4000**
has a 0 of its own. Be sure to add the same number of 0's
that you would have to cover up, and not to count a 0
from the product.

 In conversion of measurements, the student will be multiplying by 10, 100, and 1000. Provide some examples such as the following, but limit the product to numbers less than 10,000.

2 x 1<u>0</u> = 2<u>0</u>
8 x 1<u>00</u> = 8<u>00</u>
4 x 1<u>000</u> = 4<u>000</u>
34 x 1<u>0</u> = 34<u>0</u>
60 x 1<u>0</u> = 60<u>0</u>
45 x 1<u>00</u> = 45<u>00</u>
30 x 1<u>00</u> = 30<u>00</u>

 **Learning Tasks 1-2, p 10**

1.   (a) 300   (b) 1200

2.   (a) 56   (b) 560   (c) 5600
     (d) 450   (e) 320   (f) 540
     (g) 1800   (h) 1500   (i) 2800

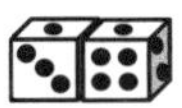 **Game**

<u>Material</u>: A set of number cards 10, 20, 30, 40, 50, 60, 70, 80, 90, 100, 200, 300, 400, 500, 600, 700, 800, 900. Another set of number cards 0, 1, 2, 2, 3, 3, 4, 4, 5, 5, 6, 6, 7, 7, 7, 8, 8, 9, 9.

<u>Procedure</u>: Shuffle the cards, keeping the cards in each set separate. Players take turns drawing one card from each set, multiplying the numbers together and writing the answer. After 3 turns the players add their products. The player with the highest sum wins the round. Play several rounds. If you run out of cards to turn over, reshuffle all the cards. If the student needs practice with multiplication facts for a particular number, such as 7, replace some of the cards with smaller numbers, such as 0, 1, or 2, with cards with those numbers.

 **Workbook Exercise 4**

Part 4 Division

(1) Division of Tens, Hundreds, and Thousands

 ➤ Divide tens, hundreds, or thousands by a 1-digit number by removing and then appending the correct number of zeros.

➤ Use **base-10 blocks**.

Discussion:	Write:
Divide 8 unit cubes into two groups	$\underline{8} \div 2 = \underline{4}$
Divide 8 tens into two groups.	$\underline{80} \div 2 = \underline{40}$
Now divide 8 hundreds into two groups.	$\underline{800} \div 2 = \underline{400}$ $\underline{8000} \div 2 = \underline{4000}$

We can cover up the 0's on the first number, either with a finger or in our minds, one at a time from the right, until we get to a number we recognize as a number that can be divided by the second number with no remainder. We then divide that number by the second number, and add back on the same number of 0's.

$$\underline{40} \div 8 = \underline{5}$$

Here, if we remove a 0 in the 40, we can't divide the 4 by 8 and get a whole number. But we can divide 40 by 8. So how many 0's do we remove from 400? (1).

$$\underline{400} \div 8 = \underline{50}$$

Can we remove 0's from the 700 to get a number we can divide by 3? (No). For this one, we will need to divide the whole number by 3, and we will get a remainder.

$700 \div 3$

$$\begin{array}{r} 233 \\ 3\overline{)700} \\ 6 \\ \overline{10} \\ 9 \\ \overline{10} \\ 9 \\ \overline{1} \end{array}$$

 **Learning Tasks 1-2, p. 11**

1.   (a) 20   (b) 300

2.   (a) 3   (b) 30   (c) 300
      (d) 20   (e) 60   (f) 40
      (g) 40   (h) 600   (i) 200

 **Workbook Exercise 5**

Practice

 **Practice 1A, p. 12**

1. (a) 93 (b) 100 (c) 102
2. (a) 198 (b) 197 (c) 72
3. (a) 33 (b) 34 (c) 5
4. (a) 1 (b) 8 (c) 1
5. (a) 120 (b) 400 (c) 1800
6. (a) 100 (b) 60 (c) 200
7. (a) 600 (b) 450 (c) 2100
8. (a) 20 (b) 80 (c) 90
9. (a) 600 (b) 240 (c) 2500
10. (a) 55 (b) 242 (c) 510 (d) 5494
11. Number of pages in 6 books = 80 x 6 = **480**
12. Number of onions in each bag = 200 ÷ 5 = **40**
13. Number sold Sunday = 70 x 4 = **280**

 **Practice 1B, p. 13**

1. (a) 150 (b) 300 (c) 180
2. (a) 20 (b) 20 (c) 200
3. (a) 540 (b) 2800 (c) 2400
4. (a) 30 (b) 40 (c) 80
5. Amount saved in 8 months = $50 x 8 = **$400**
6. Number of chocolate buns sold
   = 200 ÷ 4
   = **50**

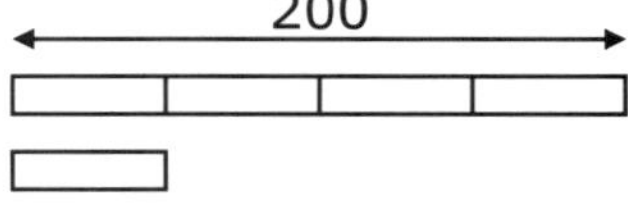

7. Total number of pears bought = 40 x 9 = **360**
8. Number of coins in 200 sets = 200 x 6 = **1200**
9. (a) Number of bags = 250 ÷ 5 = **50**
   (b) Money received = 50 x $2 = **$100**
10. (a) Total number of pens = 98 + 62 = **160**
    (b) Number of pens in each box = 160 ÷ 8 = **20**

Unit 2 Length

Part 1 Meters and Centimeters

(1) Meters and Centimeters

➢ Measure in meters and centimeters.
➢ Convert a measurement in meters and centimeters to centimeters or a measurement in centimeters to meters and centimeters.

Your student should already be familiar with the meter and the centimeter as units of length. If not, spend some time familiarizing her with the length of a centimeter and a meter using the activities at the start of this lesson. Provide opportunities for your student to estimate length in meters or centimeters. Use the term **about** when saying a length is approximately a certain number of centimeters or meters.

 Use a **ruler** for centimeter measurements and a **meter stick** for meter measurements. If you do not have a meter stick, make one from cardboard using the measurements on a ruler, or use a **measuring tape**. Show your student how to line up the 0 mark on the ruler with the beginning of the object and read the length of the object to the nearest centimeter.

Tell your student that the abbreviation for centimeter is **cm**, and the abbreviation for meter is **m**.

- ❖ Measure some objects to the nearest centimeter.
- ❖ Estimate the lengths of various objects or lines, then measure.
- ❖ Is the door about 1 m, 2 m, or 3 m tall?
- ❖ How many cm long is your thumb?
- ❖ What is the width of your thumb?
- ❖ What is the distance straight across from the tip of your thumb to the tip of your index finger when your thumb is spread out from the rest of your hand?
- ❖ What is the distance from your elbow to the tip of your fingers?
- ❖ Find something that is about 5 cm long. About 10 cm long.
- ❖ How close to 8 cm can you cut a piece of string without measuring first?
- ❖ Use a ruler to draw a line 3 cm long. 10 cm long.
- ❖ Without a ruler, draw a line 5 cm long. Then measure to see how close you came.
- ❖ Measure some objects longer than a meter and give the measurement in meters and centimeters. Write the lengths down in meters and centimeters. For example, the width of a table might be 1 m 30 cm.

Show your student on a meter stick or measuring tape that 1 m is the same as 100 cm. There are 100 cm in 1 m. Write

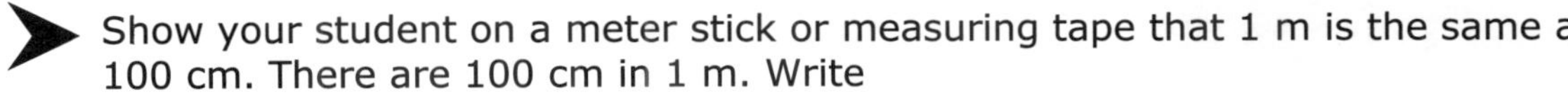

1 m = 100 cm

Ask him how many centimeters are in 2 m, or 3 m, or 9 m, or 30 m. Write

```
1 m   = 100 cm
2 m   = 2 x 100 cm    = 200 cm
3 m   = 3 x 100 cm    = 300 cm
9 m   = 9 x 100 cm    = 900 cm
30 m  = 30 x 100 cm   = 3000 cm
```

Help your student find the number of cm in a measurement given in meters and centimeters. He must convert the meters to centimeters and add that to the centimeters.

$$6 \text{ m } 45 \text{ cm} = 645 \text{ cm}$$
$$600 \text{ cm} \quad 45 \text{ cm}$$
$$645 \text{ cm}$$

Use some examples where there are less than 10 cm:

$$6 \text{ m } 5 \text{ cm} = 605 \text{ cm}$$
$$600 \text{ cm} \quad 5 \text{ cm}$$
$$605 \text{ cm}$$

➤ Write:

$$45 \text{ cm} + \underline{\qquad} = 1 \text{ m}$$

Ask your student how many more cm are needed to make 1 m. She should realize that she can use the mental math strategy of making 100, since 1 m = 100 cm.

$$45 \text{ cm} + 55 \text{ m} = 100 \text{ cm} = 1 \text{ m}$$

Give her a few more problems such as:

$$33 \text{ cm} + \underline{\qquad} = 1 \text{ m}$$

$$1 \text{ m} - 89 \text{ cm} = \underline{\qquad}$$

Ask her how long 200 cm is in meters. If you used base-10 blocks, ask her to think of twice as many flats. How many cm would that be? (200) How many hundreds are in 200? (2) How many meters are in 200 cm? In 400 cm? In 600 cm? Write

```
200 cm = 2 m
400 cm = 4 m
700 cm = 7 m
```

➤ Ask your student how long 145 cm is in meters and centimeters. The number of hundreds is the number of meters, the remainder is the number of centimeters. If necessary, you can illustrate this with base-10 blocks by using a 100-flat, four 10-rods, and 5 1-cubes. Ask her to imagine the 100-flat spread out like 10-rods side by side, and the other 4 10-rods and the 1-cubes added to that. The ten 10-rods are the same length as 1 m, and then there are 45 cm left over.

$$145 \text{ cm} = 1 \text{ m } 45 \text{ cm}$$
$$100 \text{ cm} \quad 45 \text{ cm}$$
$$1 \text{ m} \quad 45 \text{ cm}$$
$$1 \text{ m } 45 \text{ cm}$$

Ask her how many meters and centimeters are in 435 cm. There are as many meters as there are hundreds. Discuss the following or similar problems:

        145 cm = 1 m 45 cm
        435 cm = 4 m 35 cm
        702 cm = 7 m 2 cm

 **Learning Tasks 1-8, pp 15-16**

1. (a) 25   (b) 125

2. (a) 200   (b) 3

4. 145

5. (a) 190 cm   (b) 155 cm   (c) 286 cm
    (d) 289 cm   (e) 308 cm   (f) 406 cm

6. 3 m 95 cm

7. (a) 1 m 80 cm   (b) 1 m 95 cm   (c) 2 m 62 cm
    (d) 2 m 99 cm   (e) 3 m 4 cm   (f) 4 m 9 cm

8. 1 m 89 cm, 1 m 96 cm, 2 m 8 cm

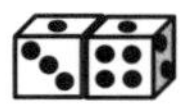 **Make 100**

<u>Material</u>: Deck of playing cards with face cards and tens removed.

<u>Procedure</u>: Shuffle and deal out all cards. Each player turns over two cards. The first card turned over is the tens, the second is the ones. The player writes down the number that makes 100 with the number formed. For example, he turns over a 5 and a 4. The number is 54, and the player writes down 46. Each player then turns over two more numbers and again makes 100 with the number formed. He then adds the two numbers he has written together. The player with the largest sum gets all the cards that have been turned over. Play continues until all cards are used. The player with the most cards wins.

Workbook Exercise 6
Allow your student to apply his problem solving abilities to problem 8. If he has trouble, suggest that he convert the m into cm. He may come up with a different strategy. Other strategies will be taught in the next section.

(2) Addition and Subtraction of Compound Units

 ➢ Add and subtract lengths in meters and centimeters.

 A number of skills and strategies can be used when adding and subtracting compound units in the metric system, including renaming, mental addition and subtraction of 2- and 3- digit numbers, and determining number pairs that make 100 (for meters and centimeters) or 1,000 (for kilometers and meters or liters and milliliters). Although addition and subtraction of compound units can be performed by converting the larger unit into the smaller and adding or subtracting with the formal algorithm, encourage your student to use mental strategies.

 Discuss the following or other problems involving addition and subtraction of compound units in meters and centimeters with your student. Start with adding or subtracting just cm without renaming cm as m, then with renaming, then adding or subtracting meters and centimeters, first without renaming, then with renaming. Discuss various strategies that can be used.

2 m 60 cm + 2 cm = 2 m 62 cm 2 m 60 cm + 25 cm = 2 m 85 cm 2 m 65 cm + 28 cm = 2 m 93 cm	Add the centimeters together.
2 m 60 cm + 67 cm $\qquad$ + 67 cm 2 m 60 cm $\longrightarrow$ 2 m 127 cm = 3 m 27 cm	Add the centimeters together. Write an intermediate step or look ahead to see that adding the centimeters will result in more than 100 cm, or an additional m.

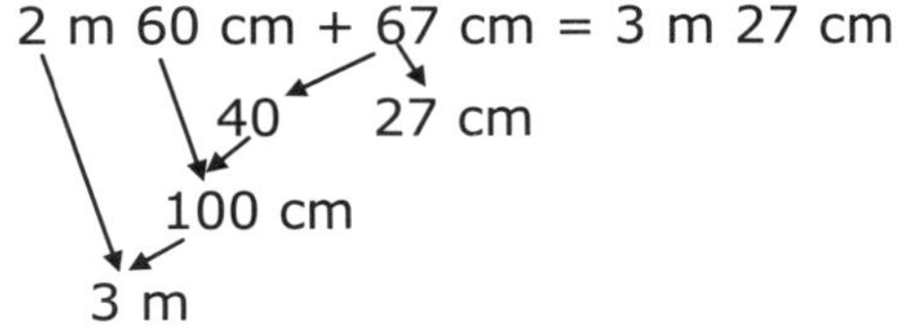

	Add the centimeters and rename 100 cm as 1 m. Or, make 100 with the centimeters.

2 m 65 cm + 23 m 28 cm $\qquad$ + 23 m $\qquad$ + 28 cm 2 m 65 cm $\longrightarrow$ 25 m 65 cm $\longrightarrow$ 25 m 93 cm	Add the meters first, then the centimeters.

32 m 75 cm + 2 m 28 cm

$$32 \text{ m } 75 \text{ cm} \xrightarrow{+ 2 \text{ m}} 34 \text{ m } 75 \text{ cm} \xrightarrow{+ 28 \text{ cm}} 35 \text{ m } 3 \text{ cm}$$

Add the meters first, then the centimeters.
Write an intermediate step or look ahead to see that adding the cm will result in another m.

32 m 75 cm + 2 m 28 cm = 35 m 3 cm
103 cm
1 m   3 cm

Add the centimeters and rename 100 cm as 1 m.

32 m 75 cm + 2 m 28 cm = 35 m 3 cm
25 cm   3 cm
1 m

Or, make 100 with the centimeters.

---

32 m 75 cm + 2 m 28 cm

$$\begin{array}{r} {}^{1}\ {}^{1}\\ 3\,2\,7\,5 \text{ cm}\\ +\ 2\,2\,8 \text{ cm}\\ \hline 3\,5\,0\,3 \text{ cm} \quad = 35 \text{ m } 3 \text{ cm} \end{array}$$

Or, rewrite as centimeters, add vertically, and rewrite again in meters and centimeters.

---

4 m 30 cm − 23 cm = 4 m 7 cm

Subtract the centimeters.

---

4 m − 65 cm

4 m − 65 cm = 3 m 100 cm − 65 cm = 3 m 35 cm

Rename 1 m as 100 cm and subtract the centimeters.

---

4 m 30 cm − 55 cm

4 m 30 cm − 55 cm = 3 m 130 cm − 55 cm = 3 m 75 cm

There are not enough centimeters to subtract 55 cm. Rename 1 m as 100 cm and subtract the centimeters.

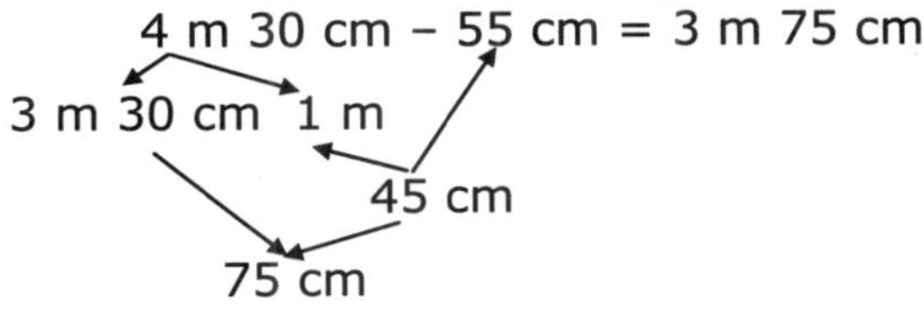

4 m 30 cm − 55 cm = 3 m 75 cm
3 m 30 cm   1 m
45 cm
75 cm

Or, subtract the centimeters from one of the meters.

---

4 m 30 cm − 2 m 28 cm = 2 m 2 cm

Subtract the meters, then the centimeters.

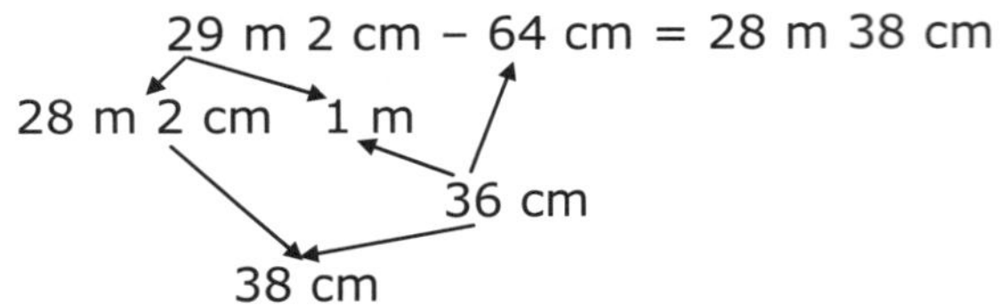

45 m 2 cm − 16 m 64 cm

$$45 \text{ m } 2 \text{ cm} \xrightarrow{\;-16\text{ m}\;} 29 \text{ m } 2 \text{ cm}$$
$$\downarrow \qquad \xrightarrow{\;-64\text{ cm}\;}$$
$$28 \text{ m } 102 \text{ cm} \longrightarrow 28 \text{ m } 38 \text{ cm}$$

29 m 2 cm − 64 cm = 28 m 38 cm

28 m 2 cm   1 m

36 cm

38 cm

Subtract the meters. Write an intermediate step or look ahead and see that there will be one less meter. Rename 1 m as 100 cm and subtract the centimeters.

Or, subtract the centimeters from one of the meters.

 **Learning Task 9, p. 17**

 **Workbook Exercise 7**

Practice

 **Practice 2A, p. 18**

1.   (a) 400 cm   (b) 140 cm   (c) 225 cm
     (d) 395 cm   (e) 405 cm   (f) 909 cm

2.   (a) 1 m 20 cm   (b) 2 m 25 cm   (c) 3 m 9 cm
     (d) 6 m 18 cm   (e) 9 m 63 cm   (f) 4 m 5 cm

3.   (a) 35 cm
     (b) 45 cm
     (c) 25 cm
     (d) 1 m 5 cm
     (e) 8 cm
     (f) 3 m 34 cm

4.   (a) 5 m 75 cm   (b) 3 m 69 cm
     (c) 3 m 91 cm   (d) 6 m 3 cm
     (e) 85 cm   (f) 5 m 14 cm
     (g) 1 m 5 cm   (h) 81 cm

5. **US➤** Ryan's height **3d➤**Rajus's height
     = 1 m 60 cm − 16 cm
     = **1 m 44 cm**

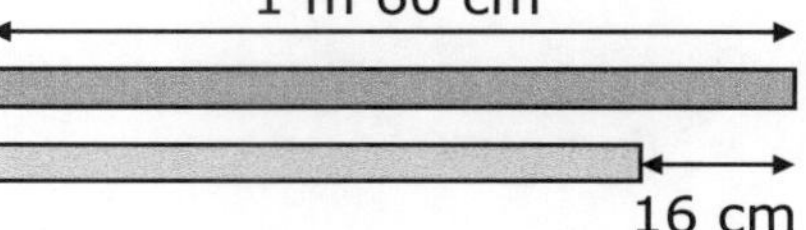

6. Total length = 1 m 80 cm + 1 m 65 cm = **3 m 45 cm**

Part 2 Kilometers

(1) Kilometers

> ➢ Understand the kilometer.
> ➢ Convert a measurement in kilometers and meters to meters and a measurement in meters to kilometers and meters.

The kilometer is the standard unit of measurement in the metric system for longer distances. In the U.S. standard system, it is the mile. A mile is longer than a kilometer. 1 km equals 0.6214 miles, or 1 mile equals 1.6093 km. So a little over half a mile (six tenths of a mile) is 1 km, 6 miles is about 10 km, and 60 miles is about 100 km. If you generally use miles, use these approximations in order to give your student an idea of what a kilometer is. For example, if the post office is a little over a mile away, you can tell your student it is about 2 km away. A town about 60 miles (or about an hours driving time) away is about 100 km away.

Page 19

Discuss some familiar distances to give your student an idea of the length of a kilometer.

Since 1 km = 1000 m, but 1 m = 100 cm, help your student avoid confusion between the conversion unit (100 or 1000) by discussing the meaning of the prefixes. The prefixes are added to the standard unit, which for length is meter. So centi- is a hundredth of the standard unit, and kilo- is a thousand times the standard unit. Tell your student:

When he sees **centi-** he should think **one hundred** times **smaller**.
A **centi**meter is **100** times **smaller** than a meter.
    100 cm → 1 **m**

When he sees **kilo-** he should think **one thousand** times **bigger**.
A **kilo**meter is **1000** times **bigger** than a meter.
    1000 **m** → 1 km

You may wish to include milli- in the discussion, since milliliter will be used in the capacity section of *Primary Mathematics 3B*. Show your student a millimeter on a ruler. There are 1000 millimeters in 1 m. The abbreviation for millimeter is mm.

When he sees **milli-** he should think **one thousand** times **smaller**.
A **milli**meter is **1000** times **smaller** than a meter.
    1000 mm → 1 **m**

➤ Write:

    455 m + _________ m = 1 km

Ask your student how many more meters are needed to make 1 km. He can use the mental math strategy of making 1000, since 1 km = 1000 m.

    455 m + 545 m = 1000 m = 1 km

Give him a few more problems such as:

    333 m + _______ m = 1 km
    1 km – 892 m = _______ m

➤ Ask your student for the equivalent number of kilometers for various thousands of meters, such as

    2000 m = _______ km
    4000 m = _______ km
    10,000 m = _______ km

The number of kilometers is the number of thousands of meters.

Write:

    2345 m

Ask your student how many thousands there are. There are 2 thousands. If that is written in kilometers, there are 345 m left.

    2345 m = 2 km 345 m

Do a few other examples, including ones where the answer gives less than a hundred meters, such as

    5002 m = 5 km 2 m
    5020 m = 5 km 20 m

➤ Write and discuss

    4 km 345 m = ___________ m

Since 4 km = 4000 m, multiply the km by 1000, then add the meters.

    4 km 345 m = 4000 m + 345 m = 4345 m

Discuss the following examples

    4 km 40 m = 4040 m   (4000 m + 40 m)
    4 km 4 m = 4004 m   (4000 m + 4 m)
    4 m 40 cm = 440 cm   (400 cm + 40 cm)
    4 m 4 cm = 404 cm   (400 cm + 4 cm)

A common error is to write 4 km 45 m as 445 m, or to not pay attention to units.

 **Learning Tasks 1-6, pp. 20-21**

1. (a) 1 km 10 m
    (b) 1 km 750 m

2. (a) 42 km; 23 km
    (b) 41 km

3. 6100 m

4. 1 km 200 m

5. (a) 1600 m   (b) 2550 m   (c) 2605 m
    (d) 3085 m   (e) 3020 m   (f) 4005 m

6. (a) 1 km 830 m   (b) 2 km 304 m   (c) 2 km 780 m
    (d) 3 km 96 m   (e) 3 km 40 m   (f) 4 km 9 m

 **Make 1000**

<u>Material</u>: Deck of playing cards with face cards and tens removed.

<u>Procedure</u>: Shuffle and deal out all cards. Each player turns over three cards. The first card turned over is the hundreds, the second is the tens, and the third is the ones. The player writes down the number that makes 1000 with the number formed. For example, he turns over a 5, a 1, and a 4. The number is 514, and the player writes down 486. Each player then turns over three more numbers and again makes 1000 with the number formed. He then adds the two together. The player with the largest sum gets all the cards that have been turned over. Play continues until all cards are used. The player with the most cards wins.

 **US➤ Workbook Exercise 8**
3d➤ Workbook Exercises 8-10

(2) Addition and Subtraction of Compound Units

 ➢ Add and subtract lengths in kilometers and meters.

 The strategies used here are similar to those used in adding and subtracting lengths in meters and centimeters. Caution the student to remember that there are 1000 m in a kilometer, but only 100 cm in a meter.

 Discuss the following or other problems involving addition and subtraction of compound units in kilometers and meters with your student. Discuss the various strategies that can be used.

600 m + 850 m	Add the meters together.
600 m + 850 m = 1450 m = 1 km 450 m	Rename 1000 m as 1 km.
600 m + 850 m = 1 km 450 m 400 m 450 m 1 km	Or, make 1000 with the meters.
2 km 965 m + 112 km 85 m + 112 m + 85 cm 2 km 965 m ⟶ 114 km 965 m ⟶ 115 km 50 m	Add the kilometers first, then the meters. Write an intermediate step or look ahead to see that adding the meters will result in another kilometer.
2 km 965 m + 112 km 85 m = 115 km 50 m 1050 m 1 km 50 m	Add the meters and rename 1000 m as 1 km.
2 km 965 m + 112 km 85 m = 115 km 50 m 35 m 50 m 1 km	Or, make 1000 with the meters.

3 km 375 m + 2 km 684 m
 	
    1   1
    3 3 7 5   m
 + 2 6 8 4   m
    6 0 5 9   m   = 6 km 59 m
	Or, rewrite as meters, add vertically, and rewrite again in kilometers and meters.

4 km 36 m – 300 m

4 km 36 m – 300 m = 3 km 1036 m – 300 m
                          = 3 km 736 m

Rename 1 km as 1000 m and subtract the meters.

4 km 36 m – 300 m = 3 m 736 m

3 km 36 m 1 km

700 m

736 m

Or, subtract the meter from a kilometer.

45 km 2 m – 6 km 360 m

45 km 2 m —— (– 6 m) → 39 km 2 m
            ↓
38 km 1002 m —— (– 360 m) → 38 km 642 m

Subtract the kilometers. Write an intermediate step or look ahead and see that there will be one less kilometer. Rename 1 km as 1000 m and subtract the meters.

39 km 2 m – 360 m = 38 km 642 m

38 km 2 m 1 km

640 m

642 m

Or, subtract the meters from one of the kilometers.

Learning Tasks 7-8, p. 22

8.   120 m

US> Workbook Exercise 9
3d> Workbook Exercise 11

Practice

 **Practice 2B, p. 23**

1. (a) 3000 m   (b) 1450 m   (c) 2506 m
    (d) 2060 m   (e) 3078 m   (f) 4009 m

2. (a) 1 km 680 m   (b) 1 km 85 m   (c) 2 km 204 m
    (d) 3 km 90 m   (e) 3 km 999 m   (f) 4 km 1 m

3. (a) 200 m
    (b) 400 m
    (c) 955 m
    (d) 960 m
    (e) 60 m
    (f) 1 km 725 m

4. (a) 5 km 650 m   (b) 3 km 510 m
    (c) 4 km 100 m   (d) 6 km
    (e) 1 km 950 m   (f) 4 km 100 m
    (g) 2 km 675 m   (h) 1 km 50 m

5. Distance = 4 km 400 m − 2 km 940 km = **1 km 460 m**

Part 3 Yards, Feet, and Inches

(1) Yards, Feet, and Inches

➢ Measure in yards, feet, and inches.
➢ Convert a measurement between yards, feet, and inches.

Yards, feet, and inches are customarily used for measuring length in the U.S. Your student will not be converting between measurement systems in *Primary Mathematics*, but it is useful for them to have an approximate idea of how they compare. 1 meter is slightly longer than a yard. A centimeter is less than half as long as an inch.
1 inch = 2.54 cm ≈ two and a half cm
1 foot = 30.48 cm ≈ 30 cm
1 yard = 0.9144 m ≈ 1 meter
1 meter = 1.0936 yards ≈ 1 yard ≈ 36 inches

➤ If necessary, familiarize your student with yards, feet, and inches using some of the introductory ideas given in section 1 for part 1 (p. 18 in this guide). Your student should have a feel for the lengths so that she can roughly estimate the lengths of objects, as well as be able to measure in those lengths. If she does not already know, explain to her that the abbreviation for inches is **in.**, for feet is **ft**, and for yards is **yd**. The plural of foot is feet; we talk about something measuring one foot or several feet. The abbreviation for both foot and feet is ft.

US➤ Page 24

➤ Give your student an idea of the relationship between the metric measurements and the standard US measurements. You can ask her to discover the answer to questions such as the following using rulers, a yard stick and a meter stick, or a tape measure.

❖ Which is longer, an inch or a centimeter? (in.)
❖ About how much longer? (About two and a half times longer / a little more than twice as long.)
❖ About how many inches are there in 10 cm? (4)
❖ In 20 cm? (8)
❖ In 30 cm? (12)
❖ About how many cm are there in a foot? (30)
❖ Which is longer, a meter or a yard? (m)
❖ How much longer? (About 9 cm or about 3 in.)

➤ Use a **ruler** and a **yard stick**. Help your student determine that 1 foot equals 12 inches and 1 yard equals 36 inches. Ask her how many feet are in 1 yd. She can count by 12's: 12, 24, 36. There are 3 feet in 1 yard.

        1 ft = 12 in.
        1 yd = 3 ft

➤ Discuss the following:

        1 ft = 1 x 12 in. = 12 in.
        2 ft = 2 x 12 in. = 24 in.
        3 ft = 3 x 12 in. = 36 in.
        6 ft = 6 x 12 in. = 72 in.
        10 ft = 10 x 12 in. = 120 in.

To find the number of inches in a given number of feet, multiply the feet by 12.

If necessary, illustrate with **linking cubes** or several **rulers**, or represent the process in a drawing, similar to the drawings used for modeling problems. Tell your student to pretend that one cube has a length of 1 inch. 12 cubes represent 1 foot. Make sets of 12, each set with a single color. 3 sets next to each other (or 3 rulers) illustrates 3 ft.

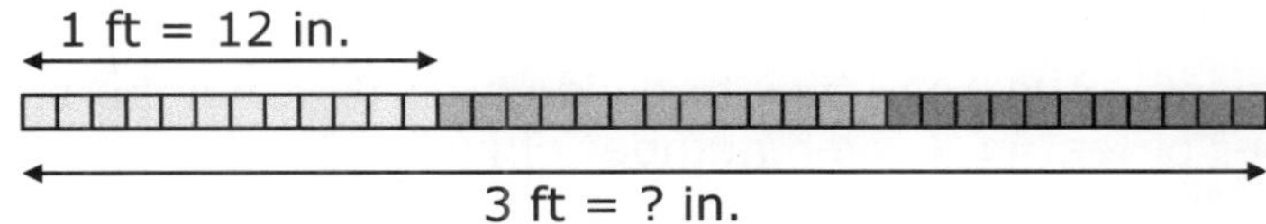

➤ Discuss the following:

        1 yd = 1 x 3 ft = 3 ft
        2 yd = 2 x 3 ft = 6 ft
        3 yd = 3 x 3 ft = 9 ft
        10 yd = 10 x 3 ft = 30 ft

To find the number of feet in a given number of yards, multiply the yards by 3.

You can illustrate this with a model showing 3 feet in a yard:

Ask your student for the number of inches in 1 yard.

        1 yd = 3 ft = 3 x 12 in. = 36 in.

➤ Discuss problems such as:

        3 ft 4 in. = 40 in.   5 yd 2 ft = 17 ft
    3 x 12 in.   5 x 3 ft
      36 in.   15 ft
            40 in.   17 ft

Multiply the feet by 12 to get   Multiply the yards by 3 to get
the number of inches in 3 ft,   the number of feet in 5 yards,
and then add the 4 inches.   and then add the 2 feet.

This can be modeled as 3 units whose value is 12, plus 4 more units whose value is 1, similar to the models used in two-step word problems in *Primary Mathematics 3A*.

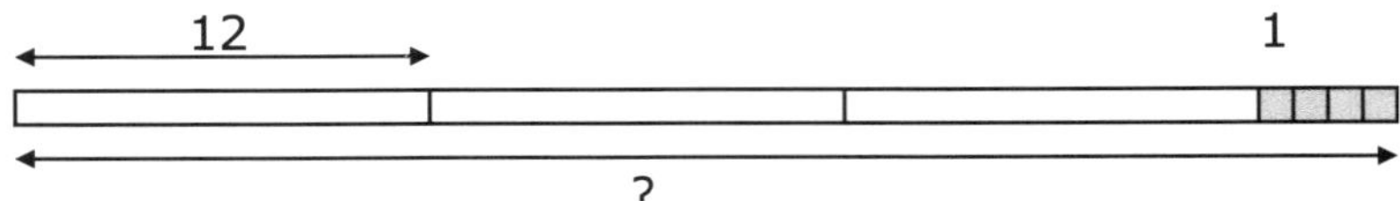

➤ Discuss the following:

3 ft = 3 ÷ 3 yd = 1 yd
6 ft = 3 ÷ 3 yd = 2 yd
12 ft = 12 ÷ 3 yd = 4 yd

To find the number of yards in a given number of feet, divide the feet by 3.

Students have not yet learned how to divide by 2-digit numbers, but they can find the number of feet in a given number of inches for easy multiples of 12 such as 24 or 36.

36 in. = 3 ft   Count by 12's to 36 – 12, 24, 36

➤ Discuss some problems such as the following.

25 ft = 8 yd 1 ft
24 ft 1 ft
8 yd

$$\begin{array}{r} 8 \\ 3\overline{)25} \\ 24 \\ \hline 1 \end{array}$$

Divide 25 by 3. The quotient is the number of yards, and the remainder the number of feet.

Ask if the answer will ever have more than 2 feet. It will not — if it does there is another yard.

Discuss some problems such as the following. Use small multiples of 12 such as 24 or 36 only, plus a few inches.

15 in. = 1 ft 3 in.
12 in. 3 in.
1 ft

Since there are 12 inches in a foot, take away 12 for one foot, which leaves 3 inches.

 **US➤ Learning Tasks 1-7, p. 25**

1.   (a) 2   (b) 5
2.   (a) 24   (b) 6
3.   35 ft
4.   5
5.   (a) 5   (b) 17
6.   (a) 84
7.   Answers will vary.

 **Additional Learning Tasks, appendix p. b1**

1.   (a) 84   (b) 36
2.   (a) 6   (b) 18
3.   (a) 4   (b) 64
4.   (a) 2   (b) 11
5.   4 yd 2 ft
6.   2 ft 6 in.
7.   47 feet

 **US➤ Workbook Exercise 10**
Exercise 10a, appendix pp. b2-b3

(2) Addition and Subtraction of Compound Units

 ➤ Add and subtract lengths in yards and feet and in feet and inches.

 The strategies used here are similar to those used in adding and subtracting metric lengths, except that 1 yard is renamed as 3 feet, and 1 foot is renamed as 12 inches. Renaming in a base other than 10 is good preparation for other instances where the base is not ten; for example, when adding hours and minutes or when adding or subtracting whole numbers and fractions. Instead of using a strategy of make a 10, we can "make a 3" in the case of yards and feet, or "make a 12" in the case of feet and inches. Instead of subtracting from a ten, we can subtract from a 3 in the case of yards and feet, or subtract from a 12 in the case of feet and inches.

 Discuss the strategies for adding in compound units.

3 ft 6 in. + 9 ft 8 in.

$$3 \text{ ft } 6 \text{ in. } \xrightarrow{+\,9\text{ ft}} 12 \text{ ft } 6 \text{ in. } \xrightarrow{+\,8\text{ in.}} 12 \text{ ft } 14 \text{ in. } = 13 \text{ ft } 2 \text{ in.}$$

Add feet first. Write an intermediate step or look ahead to see if adding the inches will result in a sum greater than 12, and therefore another foot. If it does not, write the sum for the feet and then the inches. If it does, increase the sum for the feet by 1. Add the inches. Rename 12 inches as one foot. The difference from 12 is the number of inches for the answer.

When adding feet and inches, we are working with fairly small numbers; the total for the inches will be less than 24. So your student may be able to add the inches first, see if the sum is greater than 12, find the difference from 12, keep that in mind, add the feet, add the extra foot from the inches, write down the number of feet, then write down the number of inches.

Your student might also be able to apply a strategy similar to making a 10, but making a 12 instead. 8 in. needs 4 more inches to be one foot. Take them from the 6 inches, increasing the number of feet by 1, and leaving 2 in.

3 yd 1 ft + 6 yd 2 ft

$$3 \text{ yd } 1 \text{ ft } \xrightarrow{+\,6\text{ yd}} 9 \text{ yd } 1 \text{ ft } \xrightarrow{+\,2\text{ ft}} 9 \text{ yd } 3 \text{ ft } = 10 \text{ yd}$$

Add yards first. Write an intermediate step or look ahead to see if adding the feet will result in a sum greater than 3, and therefore another yard. If it does not, write the sum for the yards and then the feet. If it does, increase the sum for the yards by 1. Add the feet. Rename 3 feet as one yard. The difference from 3 is the number of feet for the answer.

When adding yards and feet, we are working with fairly small numbers; the total for the feet will be less than 6. So the student may be able to add the feet first, see if the sum is greater than 3, find the difference from 3, keep that in mind, add the yards, add the extra yard from the feet, write down the number of yards, then write down the number of feet.

3 yd 1 ft + 6 yd 2 ft
 	
   3 yd 1 ft
+ 6 yd 2 ft
   9 yd 3 ft   = 10 yd
	The problem can also be rewritten vertically, and rewrite again in yards and feet.

3 ft – 4 in. = 2 ft 8 in. 2 ft 12 in. 8 in.	Rename 1 ft as 12 in. Write down the remaining feet. Subtract 4 in. from 12 in. Write down the difference.

15 ft 2 in. – 6 ft 10 in.
 	
    – 6 ft
15 ft 2 in. ⟶ 9 ft 2 in.
      ↓   – 10 in
  8 ft 14 in. ⟶ 8 ft 4 in.
 	
9 ft 2 in. – 10 in. = 8 ft 4 in.
8 ft 12 in.
     2 in.
   4 in.
	Subtract the feet. Write an intermediate step or look ahead and see if there will be one less foot. Rename 1 ft as 12 in. and add it to the inches in the first number, and subtract the inches.
	
	Or, subtract the inches from one of the feet.

Similar strategies can be used for subtraction of yards and feet, except that 1 yard is renamed as 3 feet.

US> Learning Task 8, p. 26

8.   (a) 6 ft 5 in.

       (b) 2 ft 9 in.

Additional Learning Tasks, appendix p. b1

1.   8 ft 6 in.

2.   1 yd 2 ft

Part 4 Miles

(1) Miles

 ➤ Add and subtract distances in miles.

 In the U.S., longer distances are measured in miles. A mile is longer than a kilometer. 1 km equals 0.6214 miles, or 1 mile equals 1.6093 km. So a little over half a mile is 1 km, 6 miles is about 10 km, and 60 miles is about 100 km. Since the student hasn't yet been introduced to 5-digit numbers or how to divide by 4-digit numbers, conversions between miles and feet will not be covered at this time.

 Tell your student we use miles in the U.S. to measure longer distances. He is probably familiar with miles. Discuss some distances in miles. You may wish to relate miles to kilometers. A mile is a little shorter than 2 kilometers.

   1 mile = 5280 feet

The abbreviation for miles is **mi**.

Miles can be added and subtracted.

 **US› Page 27 and Learning Task 1-2, p. 27**

   1. 21 mi   2. (a) 2930 mi.   1670 mi.

 Discuss the following problems:

The distance between Atlanta and Dallas is 800 miles. The distance between Atlanta and El Paso is 1450 miles. What is the distance between Dallas and El Paso?

You can have your student diagram the information:

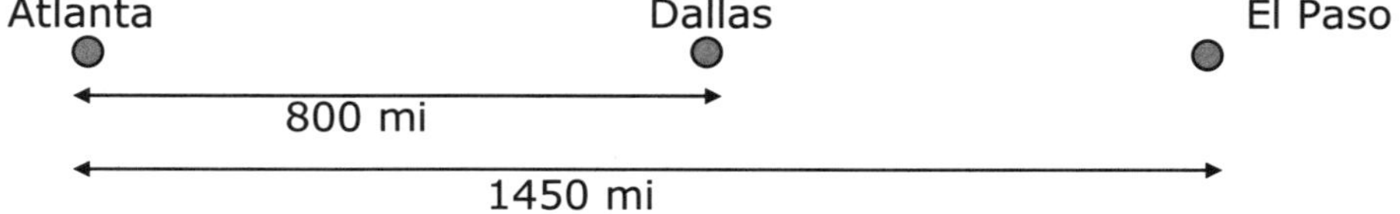

Distance between Dallas and El Paso = 1450 mi – 800 mi = 650 mi.

How many miles would you fly if you took a round trip from El Paso to Atlanta?

Total distance = 1450 mi + 1450 mi = 2900 mi

 **US› Workbook Exercise 11**
Exercise 11a, appendix pp. b4-b5

Practice

 **US> Practice 2C, p. 28**

1. (a) 15 ft   (b) 263 ft   (c) 925 ft

2. (a) 108 in.   (b) 82 in.   (c) 117 in.

3. (a) 9 yd 0 ft   (b) 36 yd 0 ft (c) 70 yd 2 ft

4. (a) 1 ft 0 in. (b) 1 ft 4 in. (c) 2 ft

5. (a) 1 ft   (b) 2 ft
    (c) 1 ft   (d) 5 in.
    (e) 4 in.

6. (a) 5 yd 2 ft
    (b) 9 yd 1 ft
    (c) 8 yd 0 ft
    (d) 1 yd 2 ft
    (e) 8 yd 2 ft
    (f) 0 yd 2 ft

7. (a) 12 ft 11 in.
    (b) 9 ft 11 in.
    (c) 12 ft 3 in.
    (d) 11 ft 5 in.
    (e) 9 ft 10 in.
    (f) 1 ft 10 in.

➤ Practice 2D (in appendix)

1. (a) 18 ft   (b) 84 in.
    (c) 34 in.   (d) 79 in.
    (e) 325 ft   (f) 131 ft

2. (a) 8 yd 1 ft   (b) 68 yd 0 ft
    (c) 104 yd 2 ft   (d) 33 yd 1 ft
    (e) 1 ft 4 in.   (f) 2 ft 2 in.

3. (a) 1 ft   (b) 4 in.
    (c) 7 in.   (d) 6 in.

4. (a) 1 ft 10 in.
    (b) 16 yd 0 ft
    (c) 10 yd 2 ft
    (d) 7 yd 2 ft
    (e) 8 ft 11 in.
    (f) 477 ft 5 in.

5. (a) <   (b) >
    (c) <   (d) =

Unit 3 Weight

Part 1 Kilograms and Grams

(1) Kilograms and Grams

- ➢ Measure in kilograms and grams.
- ➢ Convert a measurement in kilograms and grams to grams or a measurement in grams to kilograms and grams.

Your student should already be familiar with the kilogram and the gram as units of weight. This section reviews this, and introduces the student to conversion between kilograms and grams. Strictly speaking, the kilogram is a unit of mass, not weight. However, since we use the term weight in daily speech when weighing things, it will be used here.

A quart (or liter) of water weighs about 1 kg. Four hundred pennies weigh about 1 kg. A kilogram is just a little more than two pounds. A person weighing 40 kg weighs approximately 80 pounds.

Two regular paper clips weigh about 1 gram. The unit cube in some base-10 sets weigh 1 gram. A teaspoon of water weighs 5 grams. Many food products have weights in both kilograms and grams and in pounds.

If your student has not used earlier levels of *Primary Mathematics* and lives in the U.S. where kilograms or grams are not commonly used, spend some time familiarizing her with the weight of a kilogram and gram.

The abbreviation for kilogram is **kg**, and the abbreviation for gram is **g**.

Give your student practical experience in measuring weights with a **balance** and **metric weights**. Encourage her to estimate before measuring.

Remind your student that the prefix **kilo-** means 1,000 times bigger. A kilogram is 1,000 times bigger than a gram. Write

1 kg = 1000 g

Conversion between kilograms and grams is the same as between kilometers and meters.

If necessary, you can discuss the following problems:

2000 g = ______ kg	2 kg
10,000 g = ______ kg	10 kg
2345 g = ______kg ______ g	2 kg 345 g The number of kg is the thousands.
5002 g = ______ kg ______ g	5 kg 2 g
4 kg = _______ g	4 kg = 4 x 1000 g = 4000 g

4 kg 345 g = __________ g   Multiply the kg by 1000 and add the grams.
                                   4000 g + 345 g = 4345 g

4 kg 4 g = __________ g   4000 g + 4 g = 4004 g

Page US>29 3d>24
Learning Tasks 1-6, US>pp. 30-31 3d>pp. 25-26
Point out that the kilogram on the scale on the first of these pages and in
learning task 1 is divided into 10 equal parts, so each part stands for 100 g.
The kilogram on the scale in learning task 2 is divided up into 20 equal parts,
so each part stands for 50 g.

		800 g	1 kg 300 g
1.	(a)	1 kg	(b) 1 kg 200 g
	(c)	900 g	(d) 1 kg 700 g
2.		2200 g	
3.		1 kg 400 g	
4.		150 g; 150 g	
5.		chicken, 150 g	
6.	(a)	4 kg 100 g	(b) 1 kg 100 g

US> Workbook Exercises 12-13
3d> Workbook Exercises 12-14

(2) Addition and Subtraction of Compound Units

 ➢ Add and subtract weight in kilograms and grams.

 The strategies used to add and subtract weight in kilograms and grams is the same as the strategies for kilometer and meters. If necessary, you can review these strategies with your student using the problems on pages 27-28 in this guide, except that meters should be changed to grams and kilometers to kilograms.

 **Learning Task 7, US➤p. 32 3d➤p. 27**

 **US➤ Workbook Exercise 14**
3d➤ Workbook Exercise 15

Practice

 **Practice 3A, US>p. 33 3d>p. 28**

1. (a) 1456 g   (b) 2370 g   (c) 3808 g
   (d) 2080 g   (e) 1008 g   (f) 4007 g

2. (a) 2 kg 143 g   (b) 1 kg 354 g   (c) 3 kg 800 g
   (d) 2 kg 206 g   (e) 3 kg 85 g   (f) 4 kg 9 g

3. (a) 605 g
   (b) 915 g
   (c) 600 g
   (d) 940 g
   (e) 460 g
   (f) 2 kg 195 g

4. (a) 5 kg 500 g   (b) 5 kg 100 g
   (c) 5 kg   (d) 6 kg 120 g
   (e) 2 kg 810 g   (f) 3 kg 250 g
   (g) 2 kg 750 g   (h) 2 kg 95 g

5. Weight gained = 32 kg − 25 kg 750 g = **6 kg 250 g**

6. (a) Total weight = 2 kg 990 g + 4 kg 200 g = **7 kg 190 g**
   (b) Difference in weight = 4 kg 200 g − 2 kg 990 g = **1 kg 210 g**

Part 2 More Word Problems

(1) Word Problems

 Solve word problems involving measurements

 Pictorial models as a tool for solving word problems were introduced in *Primary Mathematics 3A*. Two basic types of models used are a part-whole model using one bar to represent the total, and a comparison model using two or more bars to represent the quantities being compared.

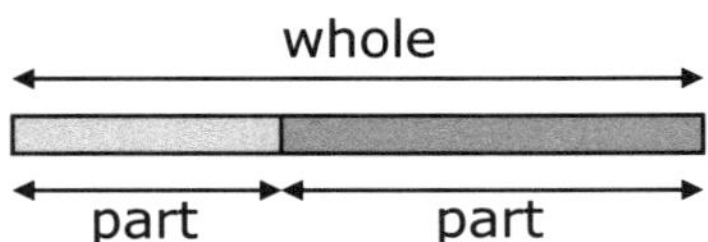

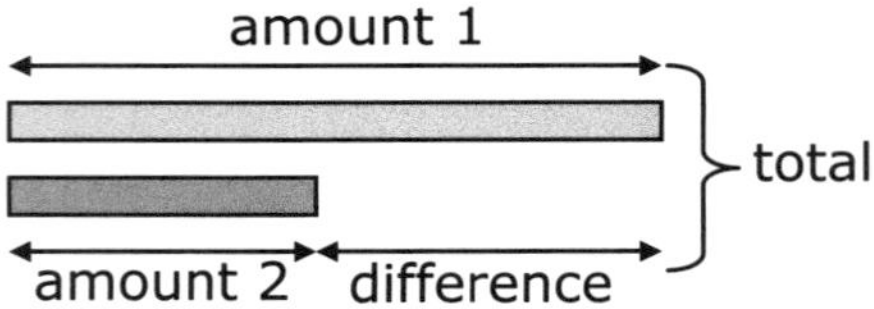

❖ Given two parts, we can find the whole by addition.
❖ Given a whole and a part, we can find the other part by subtraction.

❖ Given amount 1 and 2, we can find the difference by subtraction.
❖ Given amount 2 and the difference, we can find amount 1 by addition.
❖ Given amount 1 and the difference, we can find amount 2 by subtraction.
❖ Once both amounts have been found, we can find the total by addition.
❖ Given the total and amount 1, we can find amount 2 by subtraction, and then the difference by subtraction.

The part-whole and comparison models are also used with multiplication and division. Each part of equal value is called a unit. The comparison model is used for problems involving how many times as many or how many times more one quantity is than another.

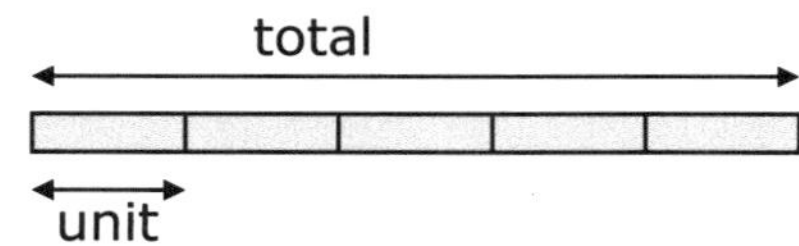

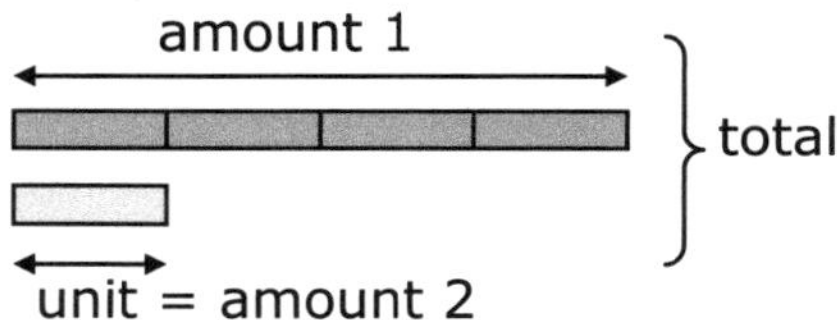

❖ Given the total and the number of units, we can find the value of a unit by division.
❖ Given the value of a unit and the number of units, we can find the total by multiplication.

❖ Given the value of the unit and how many times as much amount 1 is compared to amount 2, we can find amount 1 by multiplication.
❖ Given amount 1 and how many times as much amount 1 is compared to amount 2, we can find amount 2 by division.
❖ We can then find the difference by multiplication or subtraction, and the total by multiplication or addition.

These models can be combined to illustrate more complicated problems.

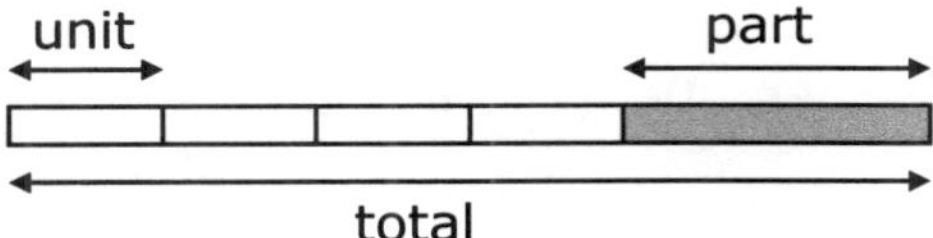

❖ Given the value of a unit, the number of units, and a part, we can find the total by multiplication and then addition.
❖ Given the value of a unit, the number of units, and the total, we can find the part by multiplication and then subtraction.
❖ Given the total, the part, and the number of units, we can find the value of the unit by subtraction, and then division.

Help your student become proficient at drawing models when needed, but do not require him to draw a model for every exercise problem.

Page 3d❯29 US❯34
Learning Tasks 1-10, US❯pp. 35-37 3d❯pp. 30-32

Discuss the learning tasks in the text. Ask your student questions to get him to talk about the problems and the models. An example of the types of questions you might ask is given for learning task 4. You may want to have your student draw the model for learning tasks 1 or 2, but he may be able to solve the problem without a diagram. Have him draw a model for learning task 10.

1.   850 g
     Weight of sauce
     = 560 g – 305 g
     = **255 g**

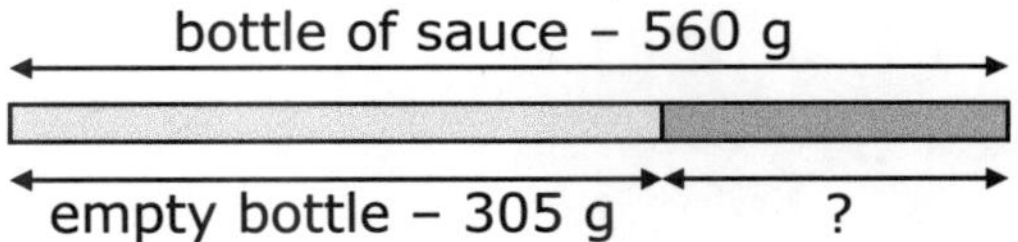

2.   Weight of fruit = Weight of basket of fruit – weight of empty basket
              = 1 kg 60 g – 200 g = **860 g**

3.   **19** kg; **19** kg

4.   **4750** g; **4 kg 750 g**
     ❖ Which one is heavier? (The watermelon.)
     ❖ How much does the papaya weigh? (950g)
     ❖ Which bar shows the weight of the papaya? (The bottom one.)
     ❖ How much does the watermelon weigh? (5 times heavier.)
     ❖ What is the unit? (The weight of the papaya.)
     ❖ How can we find the weight of the watermelon? (Multiply by 5.)
     ❖ How can we find the difference between the weight of the watermelon and the papaya? (Multiply the weight of the papaya by 4, the difference in the number of units, or subtract the weight of the papaya from the weight of the watermelon.)
     ❖ How can we find the total weight of the papaya and the watermelon? (Add the weight of the watermelon and papaya together, or multiply the weight of the papaya by 6.)

5.   **33** kg **800** g

6.   (a) Total weight = 3 kg 200 g + 1 kg 800 g = **5 kg**
     (b) Difference in weight = 3 kg 200 g − 1 kg 800 g = **1 kg 400 g**

7.   (a) **US➤** Weight of the watermelon = 2 kg 50 g + 600 g = **2 kg 650 g**
          3d➤ Weight of the jackfruit = 2 kg 50 g + 600 g = **2 kg 650 g**
     (b) Total weight = 2 kg 50 g + 2 kg 650 g = **4 kg 700 g**

8.   Weight of the salt = 2 kg 400 g − 1 kg 950 g = **450 g**

9.   **400** g

10. Drawings can vary.

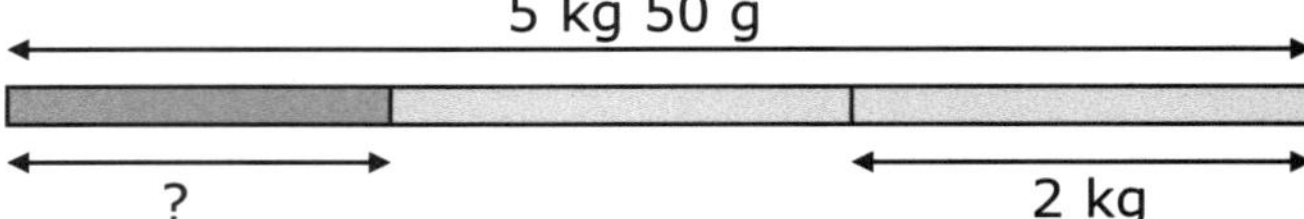

Weight of 2 packets of sugar = 2 x 2 g = **4** kg
Weight of the tin of cooking oil = 5 kg 50 g − 4 kg = **1** kg **50** g

---

US➤ Workbook Exercise 15
3d➤ Workbook Exercise 16

Practice

 **Practice 3B, US➤p. 38 3d➤p. 33**

1. (a) 5000 g (b) 1950 g (c) 1060 g
   (d) 2805 g (e) 2005 g (f) 3002 g

2. (a) 1 kg 905 g (b) 1 kg 55 g (c) 2 kg 208 g
   (d) 3 kg 390 g (e) 3 kg 599 g (f) 5 kg 2 g

3. (a) 3 kg 240 g (b) 5 kg 100 g
   (c) 2 kg 520 g (d) 2 kg 570 g

4. (a) 5 kg 70 g
   (b) 970 g

5. Sam's weight = 100 kg - 46 kg 540 g = **53 kg 460 g**

6. Son's weight = 70 kg ÷ 5 = 14 kg
   Total weight = 70 kg + 14 kg = **84 kg**
    or: 14 kg x 6 = 84 kg

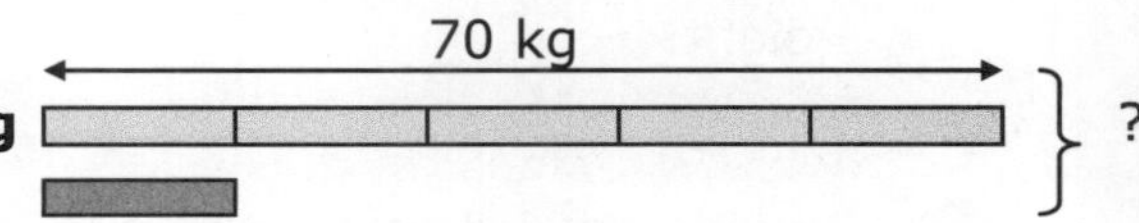

7. H's weight = 39 kg x 2 = 78 kg
   M's weight = 78 kg − 27 kg = **51 kg**

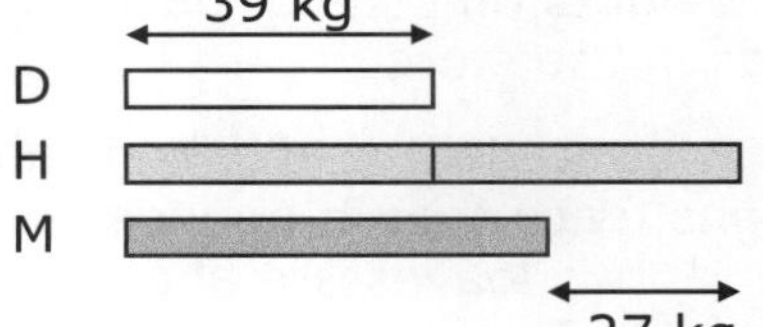

Part 3 Pounds and Ounces

(1) Pounds and Ounces

- ➢ Measure in pounds and ounces.
- ➢ Convert a measurement in pounds and ounces to ounces or a measurement in ounces to pounds and ounces.
- ➢ Add and subtract weight in pounds and ounces.

Pounds and ounces are customary units of weight in the US. They are a measure of weight, not mass. On earth, 1 kg = 2.205 pounds or 35.28 ounces, and 1 ounce = 28.35 grams. A quart of water weighs about 2 pounds.

A slice of bread, about 60 paper clips, 11 pennies, or 5 quarters weigh about one ounce.

The abbreviation for pound, lb, comes from the Latin word *libra*, a unit of weight.

Provide your student with opportunities to become familiar with the weight of pounds and ounces, and with reading scales in pounds and ounces. Point out the weights on cans or packages of food. Allow him to weigh groceries or bulk foods in the store.

Tell your student that 1 kg is about 2 pounds, so that someone who is 30 kg weighs twice that in pounds, about 60 pounds. A loaf of bread is about 1 pound, two loaves are about 1 kg. An ounce is quite a bit heavier than a gram, about 30 times heavier. 2 paper clips weigh about a gram, but 60 paper clips weigh about an ounce.

Also provide opportunities for reading various scales and determining the value of each division. You can include thermometers, dials, the speed gauge on a car, etc.

US▸Page 39

Tell your student that the abbreviation for pound is **lb**, and the abbreviation for ounces is **oz**. There are 16 ounces in a pound.

> **1 lb = 16 oz**

Ask:	Write:
How many ounces are there in 2 lb?	**1 lb = 16 oz x 1 = 16 oz** **2 lb = 16 oz x 2 = 32 oz**
In 3 lb?	**3 lb = 16 oz x 3 = 48 oz**
In 10 lb?	**10 lb = 16 oz x 10 = 160 oz**

In 3 lb 4 oz?   **3 lb 4 oz = _________ oz**

Find the number of oz in 3 lb, then add   3 lb 4 oz = **48 + 4 oz = 52 oz**
4 oz.

How can we find the number of pounds   **48 oz = __________ lb**
in 48 oz?
We can take away 16 oz for every   48 oz
pound.   ) – **16**
                                                             32 oz
) – **16**
                                                             16 oz
) - **16**
                                                             0

                                                             48 oz = 3 lb

How about 39 oz?   **39 oz = __________ lb**

When we take away 32 oz for 2 pounds,   39 oz
we are left with 7 oz.   ) – **16**
                                                             23 oz
) – **16**
                                                             7 oz

                                                             39 oz = 2 lb 7 oz

Or we can count up by 16 until we are   **1 lb = 16 oz**
going to get more than the number of   **2 lb = 32 oz**
ounces there are by adding another 16.   **3 lb = 48 oz   too much**
Then we subtract from the total number   **39 oz – 32 oz = 7 oz**
of ounces.   **39 oz = 2 lb 7 oz**

What are some ways we can add: **3 lb 10 oz + 6 lb 10 oz**

We can add the pounds first, and then   + 6 lb
the ounces. There are more than 16   3 lb 10 oz ⟶ 9 lb 10 oz
ounces, so we need to rename 16 of   ↓ + 10 oz
them as 1 lb.   9 lb 20 oz   10 lb 4 oz

                                                             1 lb 4 oz

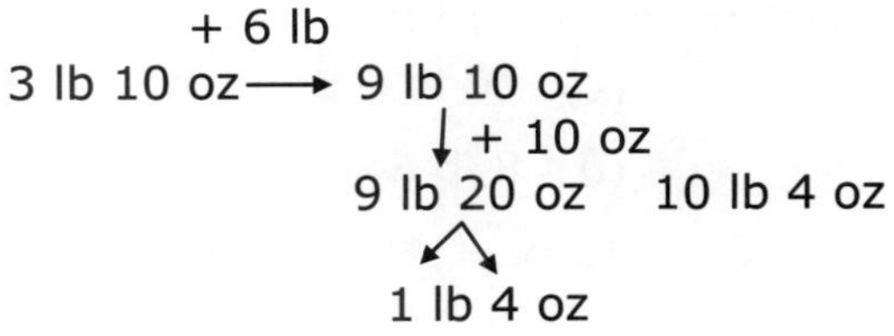

We can make 16 with the ounces by
adding 6 of the first 10 ounces to the   3 lb 10 oz + 6 lb 10 oz = 10 lb 4 oz
other 10 ounces, making 1 pound and 4
ounces.   6 oz

                                                       3 lb 4 oz   1 lb   6 lb

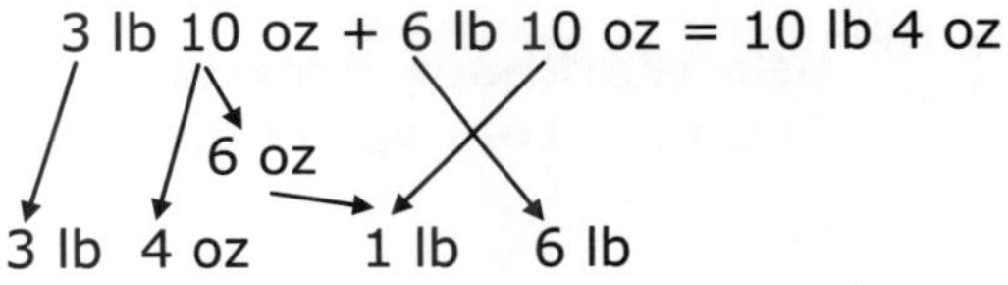

What are some ways we can subtract: **4 lb 3 oz – 2 lb 10 oz**

Subtract 2 pounds from 4 pounds, giving 2 pounds. Then subtract 10 ounces. Rename one pound as 16 ounces, giving 19 ounces, and subtract the ounces.

$$- 2\ lb$$
$$4\ lb\ 3\ oz \longrightarrow 2\ lb\ 3\ oz$$
$$\downarrow$$
$$1\ lb\ 19\ oz$$
$$\downarrow\ -\ 10\ oz$$
$$1\ lb\ 9\ oz$$

Or, after subtracting the pounds, subtract the ounces from one pound.

$$2\ lb\ 3\ oz - 10\ oz = 1\ lb\ 9\ oz$$
$$1\ lb\ 16\ oz$$

 **US>Learning Tasks 1-5, pp. 40-41**

1. (a) 2 lb   (b) 7 lb 4 oz

2. 77 oz

3. 8 oz x 3 = 24 oz = **1** lb **8** oz

4. Weight of potatoes = 6 lb 15 oz = 96 oz + 15 oz = 111 oz
The **potatoes** are lighter than the pumpkin.

5. (a) **5** lb **7** oz   (b) **1** lb **11** oz

> **Additional Learning Tasks, appendix p. b7**

1. (a) 64 oz   (b) 4 oz   (c) 68 oz

2. (a) 2 lb   (b) 2 lb 3 oz

3. (a) 10 lb 14 oz   (b) 11 lb 1 oz   (c) 14 lb 1 oz

4. (a) 10 oz   (b) 5 lb 0 oz
(c) 4 lb 15 oz   (d) 3 lb 15 oz

5. (a) 134 oz   (b) 10 lb
(c) 10 lb – 8 lb 6 oz = **1 lb 10 oz**
(d) 8 lb 6 oz + 6 lb 14 oz = **15 lb 4 oz**

6. 15 oz + 15 oz = **1 lb 14 oz**

 **US> Workbook Exercise 16**
Exercise 16a, appendix p. b9

Practice

 **Practice 3C, US>p. 42**

1. (a) 80 oz   (b) 127 oz   (c) 153 oz

2. (a) 1 lb 0 oz   (b) 1 lb 4 oz   (c) 1 lb 10 oz

3. (a) 8 lb 3 oz   (b) 9 lb 6 oz
   (c) 3 lb 14 oz   (d) 1 lb 2 oz

4. Weight of smaller watermelon = 21 lb − 12 lb 9 oz = **8 lb 7 oz**

5. Weight of avocado = 3 oz + 4 oz
                    = 7 oz
   Weight of squash = 2 x 7 oz
                    = **14 oz**

6. Weight of bananas = 21 lb ÷ 7 = 3 lb
   Total weight = 21 lb + 3 lb = **24 lb**

7. (a) Total weight = 3 lb 7 oz + 2 lb 10 oz = **6 lb 1 oz**
   (b) Difference in weight = 3 lb 7 oz − 2 lb 10 oz = **13 oz**

➤ **Practice 3D, in appendix**

1. (a) 160 oz
   (b) 127 oz
   (c) 153 oz
   (d) 1 lb 8 oz
   (e) 2 lb 1 oz

2. (a) 11 lb 4 oz
   (b) 11 lb 6 oz
   (c) 5 lb 13 oz
   (d) 12 lb 7 oz

3. (a) Total weight = 4 lb 8 oz + 2 lb 10 oz = **7 lb 2 oz**
   (b) Difference in weight = 4 lb 8 oz − 2 lb 10 oz = **1 lb 14 oz**

4. (a) Weight of cheese = 3 lb − 1 lb 12 oz = 1 lb 4 oz
        1 lb 4 oz = 20 oz
        Weight of 1 package = 20 oz ÷ 2 = **10 oz**
   (b) 1 package cost $1 or 100¢
        Cost of 1 oz = 100¢ ÷ 10 = **10¢**

Review

 **Review A, US>p. 43 3d>p. 40**

1. (a) 541   (b) 4100   (c) 3147
2. (a) 605   (b) 1724   (c) 7004
3. (a) 371   (b) 780   (c) 1628
4. (a) 29   (b) 13   (c) 54
5. 1 carton → 24 boxes
    8 cartons → 24 x 8 = **192** boxes
6. 5 people → $450
    1 person → $450 ÷ 5 = **$90**
7. Number of friends = 140 ÷ 7 = **20**
8. Total number of buttons = 46 x 8 = 368
    Number of green buttons = 368 – 200 = **168**
9. Number of unbroken bulbs = 150 – 6 = 144
    Number of boxes = 144 ÷ 4 = **36**
10. Number in 2 of the boxes = 2 x 54
                             = 108
    Total oranges = 108 + 36 = **144**

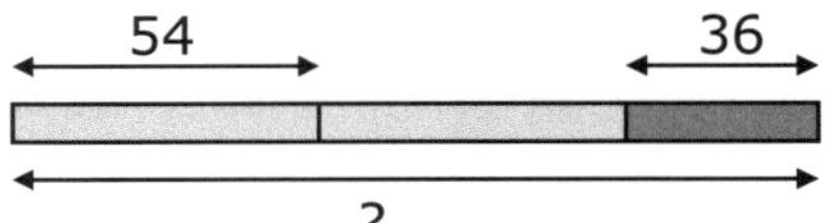

 **Review B, US>p. 44 3d>p. 41**

1. (a) 500 cm   (b) 408 cm   (c) 2560 m
    (d) 3005 m   (e) 1030 g   (f) 2080 g

2. (a) 2 m 8 cm
    (b) 3 m 20 cm
    (c) 1 km 850 m
    (d) 2 km 4 m
    (e) 3 kg 95 g
    (f) 4 kg 209 g

3. (a) 2 m 28 cm   (b) 5 m 40 cm
    (c) 65 cm   (d) 2 m 20 cm

4. (a) 6 km 210 m   (b) 10 km 200 m
    (c) 8 km 640 m   (d) 4 km 550 m

5. (a) 5 kg 45 g   (b) 8 kg 110 g
    (c) 1 kg 180 g   (d) 1 kg 795 g

6. (a) Total weight = **330 g**
    (b) Weight of pears = 330 g – 90 g = **240 g**
    (c) Weight of one pear = 240 g ÷ 2 = **120 g**

 **US> Workbook Review 1-2**

Unit 4 Capacity

Part 1 Liters and Milliliters

---

(1) Liters and Milliliters

➢ Measure in liters and milliliters.
➢ Estimate and compare capacities.

The liter as a standard unit of volume was introduced in *Primary Mathematics 2A*. In this section, the milliliter is introduced.

The amount of liquid in a container is the volume of the liquid. The **capacity** of a container is the total volume it can contain.

In the US, quart measuring cups are usually marked in both liters and quarts. A liter is slightly more than a quart (1 quart = 0.946 liters). Medicine spoons are often marked in milliliters. 1 teaspoon = 5 milliliters. Beakers and graduated cylinders can be obtained from science supply companies, but are not really required for this section if you have a quart measuring cup marked in liters.

Remind your student what a liter is by showing him a measuring cup. Show the divisions for milliliters. Tell him that we use milliliters to measure capacity less than 1 liter. There are 1,000 milliliters in a liter.

1000 ml = 1 ℓ

A milliliter is a very small amount. Show him a teaspoon and tell him that the teaspoon holds 5 ml. The amount of water that could fit inside a base-10 set unit cube is 1 ml. Ask him how many milliliters of water would fit in a 1000-cube from a base-10 set. (1,000 ml) So a 1000-cube would hold one liter of water.

Have your student use the measuring cup to first estimate and then measure the capacity of various containers in liters and milliliters. Help him determine the values for each of the divisions on the measuring cup or beaker. For example, if there is one mark between 100 and 200 ml, each division is 50 ml. He can find the volume to the nearest mark, or estimate amounts between marks. Continue to provide opportunities for reading scales.

Page US▸45 3d▸36
Learning Tasks 1-5, US▸pp. 46-48 3d▸pp. 37-39

        (a) 750 ml
        (b) 2 ℓ 300 ml

3.   2 ℓ

4.   (a) 350 ml
        (b) 800 ml
        (c) 1 ℓ 200 ml

Workbook Exercises 17-19

(2) Converting between Liters and Milliliters

 Convert a measurement in liters and milliliters to milliliters or a measurement in milliliters to liters and milliliters.

 The strategies for converting between milliliters and liters are the same as converting between grams and kilograms or meters and kilometers.

 **Learning Tasks 6-13, US>pp. 48-49 3d>pp. 39-40**

6. 1100 ml; 1 ℓ 100 ml

7. 1 ℓ 500 ml

8. (a) 1 ℓ 200 ml   (b) 2 ℓ 500 ml   (c) 2 ℓ 50 ml
    (d) 1 ℓ 5 ml   (e) 3 ℓ 400 ml   (f) 3 ℓ 105 ml

9. (a) 2000 ml   (b) 2350 ml

10. (a) 1800 ml   (b) 1080 ml   (c) 1008 ml
    (d) 3025 ml   (e) 2005 ml   (f) 3500 ml

11. 250 ml x 5 = 1250 ml = 1 ℓ 250 ml

12. 350 ml

13. Your student can either convert A to milliliters or B to liters and milliliters and then subtract.
    A can hold **260 ml** more water.

 **Workbook Exercises 20-21**

(3) Addition and Subtraction of Compound Units

 Add or subtract volume in liters and milliliters.

 The strategies for adding and subtracting milliliters and liters in compound units are the same as those for grams and kilograms or meters and kilometers.

 **Learning Task 14, US>p. 50 3d>p. 41**

 **US> Workbook Exercise 22**
3d> Workbook Exercises 22-23

Practice

Practice 4A, US>p. 51 3d>p. 42

1. (a) 3000 ml   (b) 1200 ml   (c) 2055 ml
    (d) 2650 ml   (e) 3065 ml   (f) 4005 ml

2. (a) 5 ℓ   (b) 1 ℓ 600 ml   (c) 2 ℓ 250 ml
    (d) 3 ℓ 205 ml   (e) 2 ℓ 74 ml   (f) 1 ℓ 9 ml

3. (a) more than
    (b) equal to
    (c) less than
4. (a) 2 ℓ   (b) 4 ℓ
    (c) 4 ℓ 50 ml   (d) 9 ℓ 140 ml
    (e) 1 ℓ 20 ml   (f) 2 ℓ 150 ml
    (g) 2 ℓ 720 ml   (h) 3 ℓ 925 ml
5. (a) Container A
    (b) Container B
    (c) 8 ℓ 30 ml

Practice 4B, US>p. 52 3d>p. 43

1. (a) Total = 2 ℓ 650 ml + 5 ℓ 300 ml = **7 ℓ 950 ml**
    (b) Difference = 5 ℓ 300 ml - 2 ℓ 650 ml = **2 ℓ 650 ml**

2. Amount of water in Y = 2 ℓ 800 ml + 1 ℓ 600 ml = **4 ℓ 400 ml**

3. Capacity = 2 ℓ x 9 = **18 ℓ**

4. Capacity of tank = 5 x 6 ℓ = **30 ℓ**

5. Number needed = 24 ℓ ÷ 3 ℓ = **8**

6. Amount of water still needed = 8 ℓ - 4 ℓ 650 ml = **3 ℓ 350 ml**

7. Total paint bought = 3 ℓ x 6 = 18 ℓ
    Paint used = 18 ℓ - 2 ℓ 400 ml = **15 ℓ 600 ml**

Part 2 Gallons, Quarts, Pints, and Cups

(1) Gallons, Quarts, Pints, and Cups

> ➢   Measure in gallons, quarts, pints, and cups.
> ➢   Convert between measurements.
> ➢   Add and subtract in compound units.

Gallons, quarts, pints, and cups are customary units of measurement in the US, particularly in cooking recipes. Give your student opportunities to measure, double, convert, and work with these quantities. 1 liter = 1.057 quarts

The strategies used in converting between measurements and adding and subtracting compound units are similar to those used with other measurements, except that the conversion unit is different. In working with gallons and quarts, we multiply or divide by 4 to convert, and can make a 4 or subtract from a 4 when adding and subtracting gallons and quarts. In working with quarts and pints, or with pints and cups, the conversion unit is 2.

You may want to extend the discussion presented below to tablespoons and teaspoons. There are 3 teaspoons in a tablespoon and 16 tablespoons in a cup.

Your student probably has some familiarity with gallons, quarts, pints, and cups. Obtain some containers for these amounts and show her their relative sizes. Measuring cups, such as a 4-cup measuring cup, will usually mark the quarts, but pints are not likely to be marked. Use a **gallon jug** and some **measuring cups** and have her determine how many cups are needed to fill the quart measuring cup, and how many quarts are needed to fill the gallon jug.

Teach the abbreviation for cups (c), pints (pt), quart (qt), and gallon (gal)

Tell your student that one liter is almost the same as 1 quart.

Write:

    1 pt = 2 c
    1 qt = 2 pt
    1 gal = 4 qt

Use some **linking cubes**. Use one color for cups and tell her one cube represents a cup. Use another color and make a 2-block length. This represents pints. Ask her how many blocks she would need to show 1 qt. She needs two 2-block pint pieces, or 4 blocks. Use another color and make a 4-block length to represent quarts. Ask her how many she would need to represent a gallon. She needs 4 4-block quart pieces, or 16 blocks. Put 16 blocks of a new color together to represent a gallon. Ask her how many pints are in a gallon. Since juice or milk can be bought in half-gallons, ask her how many quarts are in a half-gallon.

1 cup

1 pint

1 quart

1 gallon

Write

    1 qt = 2 pt = 4 c
    1 gal = 4 qt = 8 pt = 16 c

You can also use legos™. A piece with 1 knob represents a cup, a piece with 2 knobs represents a pint, a piece with 4 knobs represents a quart, and a piece with 16 knobs represents a gallon.

Use the linking cubes or legos™ as an aid in conversion problems and addition and subtraction of compound units involving cups, pints, quarts, and gallons.

➤ Discuss problems such as the following:

5 pt 1 c = 11 c

    1 pt = 2 c
    5 pt = 5 x 2 c = 10 c
    10 c + 1 c = 11 c
    Multiply the pints by 2 and add the cups.

15 pt = 7 qt 1 pt

    1 qt = 2 pt
    Divide the cups by 2. The quotient is the number of pints and the remainder is the number of cups.

2 gal 3 qt = 11 qt

    1 gal = 4 qt
    2 gal = 2 x 4 qt = 8 qt
    2 gal 3 qt = 8 qt + 3 qt = 11 qt
    Multiply the gallons by 4 and add the quarts.

3 pt 1 c + 7 pt 1 c = 11 pt

    Add the pints. Add the cups. Convert the cups to pints.

7 gal 2 qt − 3 gal 3 qt = 3 gal 3 qt

    Subtract the gallons, and then the quarts. To subtract quarts, rename a gallon as 4 quarts, or subtract from a 4 and add the difference to the 2 qt.

1 gal = 8 pt

    Convert first to quarts, then to pints.
    1 gal = 4 qt
    4 qt = 4 x 2 pt = 8 pt

 **US▸Learning Tasks 1-8, pp. 53-55**

2.   4 cups

3.   5 qt = 1 gal 1 qt

4.   19 gal 2 qt

5.   7 qt 1 pt

6.   10 pt 1 c

7.   2 qt 1 pt

8.   6 pt 0 c

 **Additional Learning Tasks, appendix p. b10**

1.   2 cups

2.   2 pints; 4 cups

3.   16 cups

4.   (a) 3   (b) 7

5.   (a) 2   (b) 8   (c) 2   (d) 2 qt 1 pt

6.   (a) 1 gal 1 qt
     (b) 1 gal 1 qt = 16 c + 4 c = **20 c**

 **Change it**

<u>Material</u>: **Playing cards** with face cards removed or 4 sets of number cards 1-10. 5 cards each with **gal**, **qt**, **pt**, and **c** written on them – 20 unit cards total. (Make 20 cards for 2 players. If there are 3 players make 6 cards of each; if there are 4 players make 7 cards of each, etc.)

<u>Procedure</u>: Shuffle the number cards and deal all out. Shuffle the unit cards and place them in the middle. Each player turns over a number card and two unit cards from the middle. The player must convert the number from the largest volume unit to the smallest. For example, the player turns over a 4, a **c** and a **qt**. She must convert 4 qt to cups. The result is 16. The player with the highest result gets all the playing (number) cards that have been turned over. Unit cards are put in a discard pile. The play continues until all number cards have been turned over – when all the unit cards have been turned over they are shuffled and placed upside down again. The player with the most cards at the end wins.

 **US▸ Workbook Exercise 23**
Exercise 23a (appendix pp. b11)

Practice

 **Practice 4C, US▸p. 57**

1. (a) 16 c   (b) 31 c

2. (a) 14 pt   (b) 23 pt

3. (a) 40 qt   (b) 93 qt

4. (a) >
    (b) >
    (c) =

5. (a) 11 qt 0 pt
    (b) 4 gal 3 qt
    (c) 72 pt 1 c

6. Amount B holds = 13 gal – 7 gal 1 qt = **5 gal 3 qt**

7. Pints needed = 2 qt – 1 pt = 4 pt – 1 pt = **3 pt**

8. Amount she drinks in a week = 2 c x 7 = 14 c = **7 pt**

▸ **Practice 4D, in appendix**

1. (a) 20   (b) 17
    (c) 14   (d) 25
    (e) 48   (f) 22

2. (a) <
    (b) >
    (c) =

3. (a) 14 qt 0 pt
    (b) 86 gal 3 qt
    (c) 24 pt 1 c

4. Amount of milk left = 6 gal – 3 gal 1 qt = **2 gal 3 qt**

5. Total milk = 2 c x 14 = 28 c = **7 qt**

6. Water needed = 1 gal – 1 pt = 8 pt – 1 pt = **7 pt**

7. Capacity in gallons = 84 ÷ 4 = **21 gal**

Review

 **Review C, US>p. 57 3d>p. 44**

1. (a) 5932   (b) 6808   (c) 3600

2. (a) 999   (b) 2924   (c) 5336

3. (a) 308   (b) 657   (c) 615

4. (a) 450   (b) 136   (c) 64 r6

5. Number of pens = \$504 ÷ \$8 = 63

6. Amount spent = \$628 + \$1485 = \$2113
   Total = \$2113 + \$515 = **\$2628**

7. Cookies in each box = 12 + 8 = 20
   Total cookies = 20 x 4 = **80**

8. Number of boxes sold this month = 337 + 299 = 636
   Total boxes sold = 636 + 337 = **973**

9. (a) Number of cakes = 200 ÷ 8 = 25
   (b) Money received = 25 x \$10 = **\$250**

Unit 5 Graphs

Part 1 Bar Graphs

(1) Bar Graphs I

> ➢ Read and interpret bar graphs.
> ➢ Read half scales.
> ➢ Solve problems using information from bar graphs.

In *Primary Mathematics 2*, the student learned to read and interpret picture graphs where one picture represents more than one item. This is reviewed here, and the pictures are replaced with a bar graph and a scale on one of the axes. Here the students read and evaluate bar graphs; construction of bar graphs will be taught in Primary Mathematics 4.

➤ Use **linking cubes** and **coins or other objects**. Use different amounts of each type of object, up to 10, some even and some odd amounts, for example 8 pennies, 5 nickels, 7 dimes, and 6 quarters. Your student counts the objects. He uses a linking cube to represent each object and construct a picture graph based on a scale of 1 linking cube for 1 object by placing the cubes for each type of object one above the other on some paper or a white board. You draw a horizontal line under the columns and write the object type below each column. He sticks the cubes together. You draw a vertical line beside the columns, and draw a line horizontally from the top of each cube to the vertical line. He traces the outline of the blocks, and then removes them. Tell him that this kind of graph is called a bar graph. Relate the height of the bar to the scale on the vertical line. Ask him what he would do if each linking cube represented two items. For an odd number of objects, he would have to use a half of a cube to stand for one object. Erase the odd numbers from the vertical scale, and every other horizontal line. An odd number of items would have a bar which ended half way between two marks on the scale.

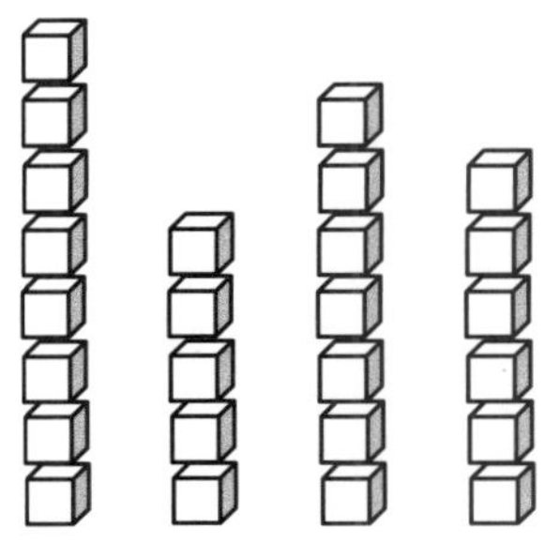 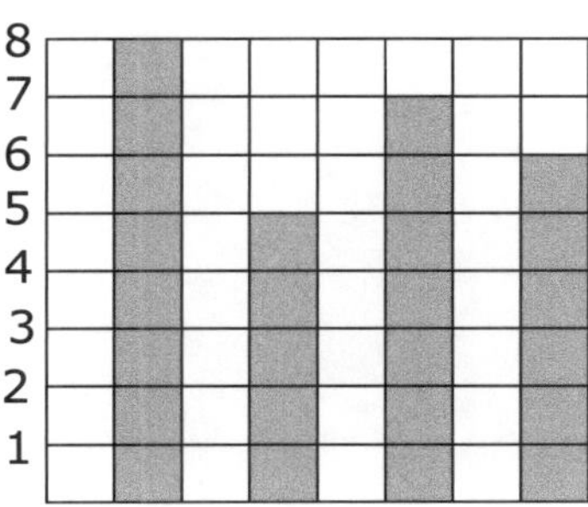 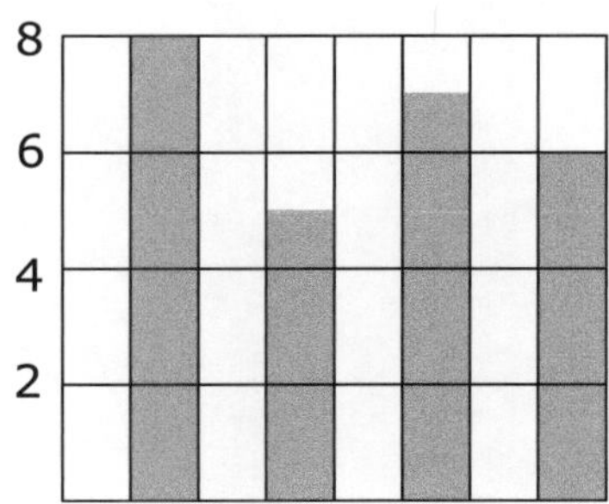

Pages US▸58-59 3d▸45-46
Ask your student for the scale on the first page. Each square stands for 2 fish.
Point out the half square. How many fish did this boy catch? (9) Show him the
bar graph on the next page. Point out that the scale on the vertical axis is 2.
Discuss the height of each bar with respect to the scale.

3d▸ Minghua - **4**; Rohan - **6**; Samy - **2**; Yonghua – **9**
Total fish = 4 + 6 + 2 + 9 = **21**
Minghua caught 4 – 2 = **2** more than Samy
Minghua caught 6 – 4 = **2** fewer fish than Rohan
Yonghua caught the most fish.
Samy caught the fewest fish.

US▸ Matthew - **4**; Pablo - **6**; Sam - **2**; Tyrone – **9**
Total fish = 4 + 6 + 2 + 9 = **21**
Matthew caught 4 – 2 = **2** more than Sam
Matthew caught 6 – 4 = **2** fewer fish than Pablo
Tyrone caught the most fish.
Sam caught the fewest fish.

Learning Tasks 1-2, US▸ pp. 60-61 3d▸ pp. 47-48
Discuss the height or length of each bar with respect to the scale. Your student
should be able to determine what each division and therefore half-division on
the scale represents.

1. (a) 75   (b) 80   (c) 5
3d▸ (d) Mathematics, Malay
US▸ (d) Mathematics, Social Studies
     (e) Science   (f) Science   (g) English

2. (a) 20   (b) 40   (c) July   (d) June
     (e) June   (f) $125

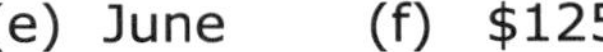

Workbook Exercise 24

(2) Bar Graphs II **US▸**(pp. 62-63) **3d▸**(pp. 49-50)

 ➢ Read scales on bar graphs.

 In this section, the student will use the scale on the axis to read the height or length of each bar.

 **Learning Tasks 3-4, US▸pp. 62-63 3d▸pp. 49-50**
Have your student determine the value for each division on the scale of the axis before answering the questions. For learning task 3 each division represents 5 books. For learning task 4 each division represents 10 visitors.

3. (a) 60   (b) 75   (c) 25   (d) Hassan
    (e) David   (f) Mary

4. (a) 320   (b) 190   (c) Wed.   (d) Thu.
    (e) Tue.   (f) 120

 **Workbook Exercise 25**

 **Workbook Review 3**
Workbook Review 4

Unit 6 Fractions

Part 1 Fraction of a Whole

(1) Fractions of a Whole

> ➤ Understand fractional notation.
> ➤ Recognize and represent fractions of a whole.
> ➤ Read and write fractions in words
> ➤ Find two fractions that make a whole.
> ➤ Understand the terms **numerator** and **denominator**.

In *Primary Mathematics 2B* the student learned to understand and write fractional notation and to find sums of fractions that make a whole. This section is primarily review. The terms **numerator** and **denominator** are introduced here.

The **denominator** gives the number of equal parts the whole is divided into. The **numerator** gives the number of equal parts represented by the fraction.

The denominator also indicates the size of the part; the larger the denominator the smaller the size since the whole is divided up into more parts. In 4 centimeters, the number of parts is 4, and centimeters is the size of each part. In $\frac{4}{7}$, the number of parts is 4, and $\frac{1}{7}$ of the whole is the size of each part. $\frac{4}{7}$ means 4 one-sevenths of a whole.

In this level, the whole is one whole unit, e.g. one pie, one apple, one circle, one length of a bar. In *Primary Mathematics 4*, the student will learn that the whole can be a group, such as 16 people, so that $\frac{1}{2}$ of the whole is 8. A larger denominator still indicates a smaller size; $\frac{1}{4}$ of 16 is 4.

Write a fraction, such as $\frac{1}{4}$, and ask your student to draw a picture showing what this fraction means. He may draw any shape, divide it up into four equal parts, and color one part. If necessary, remind him that this means one out of four equal parts. Ask him for the name of the fraction (one fourth). Tell him that the top number is called the numerator, and the bottom number is called the denominator. You can define them:
The **denominator** gives the number of equal parts the whole is divided into.
The **numerator** gives the number of equal parts represented by the fraction.
Ask him to write the fraction that would show you how many more fourths would make a whole ($\frac{3}{4}$). Ask him for the numerator and the denominator. Ask him how many fourths are in a whole. Use fraction circles and unlabeled bars (in the

appendix), shade parts of them, and ask him to name and write the fraction showing the fraction that is shaded and the fraction that is unshaded. You do not need to color in contiguous parts. Write a fraction and have him color in the amount and name and write the fraction that would make a whole.

> You can also use **linking cubes** of two different colors to represent a fraction. For example, link 4 yellows with 3 reds and ask to name and write the fraction of the bar that is yellow ($\frac{4}{7}$) 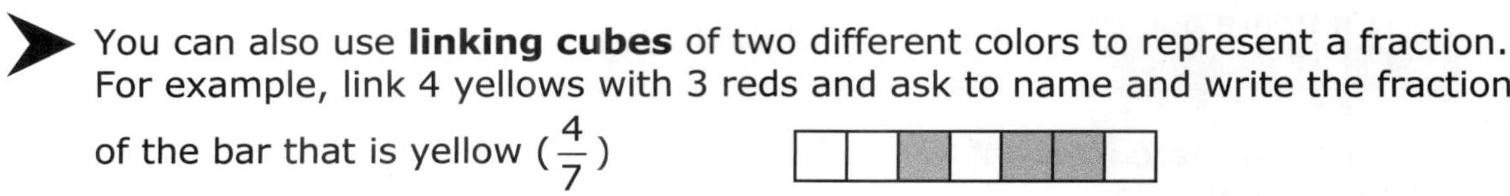

Page 3d►51, US►64
Learning Tasks 1-4, 3d►pp. 52-54 US►pp. 65-67

1. (a) 2; 5; two   (b) 3; 5; three   (c) five; 5

2. (a) $\frac{5}{8}$ (b) eight; 8   (c) $\frac{5}{8}$

3. (a) $\frac{1}{5}$ (b) $\frac{1}{6}$ (c) $\frac{1}{12}$ (d) $\frac{2}{3}$

    (e) $\frac{2}{5}$ (f) $\frac{5}{6}$ (g) $\frac{7}{8}$ (h) $\frac{7}{10}$

4. (a) 2 is the numerator, 5 is the denominator
    (b) 4 is the numerator, 10 is the denominator
    (c) 6 is the numerator, 7 is the denominator
    (d) 6 is the numerator, 9 is the denominator.

 **Make a whole**

Material
Write the following fractions on index cards:

$$\frac{1}{2}, \frac{1}{2}, \frac{1}{3}, \frac{2}{3}, \frac{1}{4}, \frac{2}{4}, \frac{2}{4}, \frac{3}{4}, \frac{1}{5}, \frac{2}{5}, \frac{3}{5}, \frac{4}{5}, \frac{1}{6}, \frac{2}{6}, \frac{3}{6}, \frac{3}{6}, \frac{4}{6}, \frac{5}{6},$$

$$\frac{1}{7}, \frac{2}{7}, \frac{3}{7}, \frac{4}{7}, \frac{5}{7}, \frac{6}{7}, \frac{1}{8}, \frac{2}{8}, \frac{3}{8}, \frac{4}{8}, \frac{4}{8}, \frac{5}{8}, \frac{6}{8}, \frac{7}{8}, \frac{1}{9}, \frac{2}{9}, \frac{3}{9}, \frac{4}{9},$$

$$\frac{5}{9}, \frac{6}{9}, \frac{7}{9}, \frac{8}{9}, \frac{1}{10}, \frac{2}{10}, \frac{3}{10}, \frac{4}{10}, \frac{5}{10}, \frac{5}{10}, \frac{6}{10}, \frac{7}{10}, \frac{8}{10}, \frac{9}{10}$$

Procedure
Shuffle the cards and place face down. Place the top two cards face up on the table. Players take turns drawing cards. If the player can match his card to a card on the table to make a whole, he keeps both cards. If not, he places the card he drew face up on the table. Play continues until all cards have been turned over. The player with the most cards wins.

 **Workbook Exercises 26-28**

(2) Comparing Fractions

> ➤ Compare and order unit fractions.
> ➤ Compare and order fractions with a common numerator.
> ➤ Compare and order fractions with a common denominator.

Unit fractions are fractions with 1 in the numerator. The student learned how to compare and order unit fractions in *Primary Mathematics 2B*. This is reviewed here, and extended to fractions with a common numerator (such as $\frac{5}{6}$ and $\frac{5}{9}$) and fractions with a common denominator (such as $\frac{4}{8}$ and $\frac{7}{8}$).

Use **fraction strips**. You can copy the ones in the appendix, glue to tagboard or a manila folder, color the different strips different colors, and cut each fraction out, or you can use commercially available fraction strips. If you are following the procedures given below, cut out pieces for $\frac{2}{4}$, $\frac{2}{6}$, $\frac{3}{6}$, $\frac{5}{6}$, and two for $\frac{1}{4}$ and for $\frac{1}{6}$.

Hand your student the pieces for $\frac{1}{4}$ and $\frac{1}{6}$, and ask her which is the smallest.

Draw her attention to the denominators. Ask her what the denominators mean. They show the number of parts of the whole, or how many pieces the whole was cut up into. If the whole is divided up into 6 parts, each part would have to be smaller than if the whole were divided up into 4 parts. So the smallest fraction is the fraction with the largest denominator, because each part, or piece, has to be smaller.

Give her two of each of the fractions, so she has two $\frac{1}{4}$'s and two $\frac{1}{6}$'s. Have her put them together and compare then. The two $\frac{1}{6}$'s together are smaller than the two $\frac{1}{4}$'s since the two pieces are smaller. Write $\frac{1}{4} + \frac{1}{4} = \frac{2}{4}$ and $\frac{1}{6} + \frac{1}{6} = \frac{2}{6}$.

Give her the $\frac{2}{4}$ piece and the $\frac{2}{6}$ piece. Write the fractions. Ask her which fraction is smaller.

When the numerators of two fractions are the same, the smaller fraction is the one with the larger denominator, since the size is smaller.

$\frac{2}{6}$ is 2 sixths, $\frac{2}{4}$ is 2 fourths, a sixth is smaller than a fourth.

➤ Give your student the fraction strips $\frac{2}{6}$, $\frac{3}{6}$, and $\frac{5}{6}$ and ask her to put them in order from smallest to largest. Write down the fractions. Point out that here, each piece is the same size, but this time there are different amounts of the same size piece.

When the denominators are the same, the smallest fraction is the one showing the fewest number of pieces, which is the one with the smallest numerator. $\frac{2}{6}$ is 2 sixths, $\frac{3}{6}$ is 3 sixths. The first one has fewer sixths.

Do other examples if necessary.

➤ Write the following fractions and see if your student can put them in order from smallest to largest: $\frac{5}{6}$, $\frac{3}{8}$, $\frac{5}{8}$. She could compare first $\frac{5}{6}$ and $\frac{5}{8}$ to show that for the two of them, the order is $\frac{5}{8}$, $\frac{5}{6}$. Since $\frac{3}{8}$ is smaller than $\frac{5}{8}$, it comes first, so the final order is $\frac{3}{8}$, $\frac{5}{8}$, $\frac{5}{6}$.

 **Learning Tasks 5-10, US➤pp. 67-68 3d➤pp. 54-55**
Illustrate learning task 10 with fraction strips, if necessary.

5. $\frac{1}{3}$

6. $\frac{3}{4}$

7. $\frac{5}{8}$

8. $\frac{3}{10}$; $\frac{3}{5}$

9. $\frac{3}{9}$; $\frac{7}{9}$

10. (a) $\frac{1}{7}$, $\frac{1}{5}$, $\frac{1}{3}$ (b) $\frac{2}{9}$, $\frac{2}{7}$, $\frac{2}{3}$

    (c) $\frac{4}{8}$, $\frac{5}{8}$, $\frac{7}{8}$ (d) $\frac{4}{12}$, $\frac{5}{12}$, $\frac{9}{12}$

 **Workbook Exercises 29 and 30**

Practice

 **Practice 6A, US▸p. 69 3d▸p. 56**

1. (a) $\dfrac{3}{4}$ (b) $\dfrac{7}{10}$ (c) $\dfrac{5}{12}$

2. (a) 2   (b) 6   (c) 9

3. (a) 8   (b) 9   (c) 10

4. (a) $\dfrac{4}{5}$ (b) $\dfrac{1}{4}$ (c) $\dfrac{3}{5}$

5. (a) $\dfrac{3}{10}$ (b) $\dfrac{1}{10}$ (c) $\dfrac{2}{9}$

6. (a) $\dfrac{5}{7}$ (b) $\dfrac{1}{2}$

7. (a) $\dfrac{1}{6}$ (b) $\dfrac{3}{10}$

Part 2 Equivalent Fractions

(1) Equivalent Fractions by Multiplication

- Understand equivalent fractions.
- Find an equivalent fraction by multiplying the numerator and denominator by a constant.

The concept of equivalent fraction is introduced here. Bars are used as one way of representing fractions. In later levels of Primary Mathematics, the student will see an analogy between a fraction bar and the part-whole bar they have learned to use in solving word problems. Each fraction, represented by one part of the fraction bar, can be considered a unit, since they are equal.

 **Page US➤ 70 3d➤ 57**

Following is a suggested discussion. Adapt as needed.

Use four separate strips of paper of equal length. You can cut an index card into fourths lengthwise.

How many parts does each piece have? (1)
We have one piece out of 1, and we can write it as $\frac{1}{1}$.

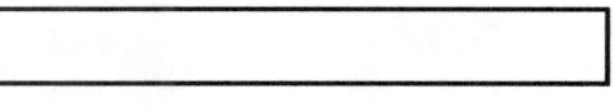

Fold one piece in half.
How many parts does this one have? (2)
What fraction is each part? (one half)
How many halves are there in one whole? (2) How many parts do we need to have a whole? (2)

We need 2 parts out of 2. We can write it as $\frac{2}{2}$.

Is $\frac{1}{1}$ equal to $\frac{2}{2}$? (Yes)

For the second strip, we have twice as many parts, but each part is half as big.

Fold another piece in half, and half again.
How big is each part? (one fourth)
How many fourths are there in a whole? (4)
Color half of the strip showing halves, and half of the strip showing fourths.
What is the fraction that is colored in each strip?

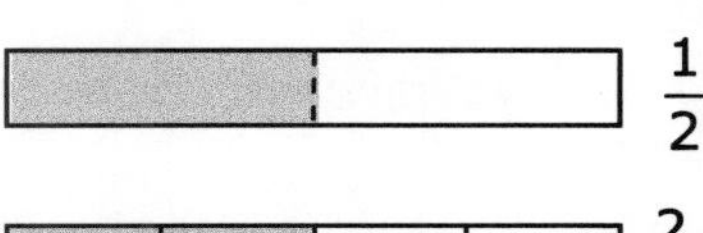

($\frac{1}{2}$ and $\frac{2}{4}$) Is $\frac{1}{2}$ equal to $\frac{2}{4}$? (Yes)

They are called **equivalent fractions**.
They have a different numerator and denominator, but they are the same.
What do you notice about the numerator and the denominator? In $\frac{2}{4}$ both the numerator and the denominator are 2 times the numerator and denominator in $\frac{1}{2}$.

When the number of total parts is multiplied by 2, the number of shaded parts is also multiplied by 2.

$$\frac{1}{2} = \frac{2}{4}$$

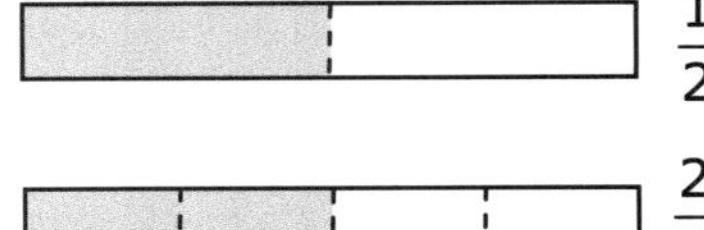

Fold another piece in half, half again, and half again. How big is each part? (one eighth)
How many eighths are there in a whole? (8)
Color half of the strip.

What fraction is colored? ($\frac{4}{8}$)

You have divided each part in half so there are twice as many parts as with $\frac{2}{4}$, but you need twice as many eighths as fourths to have the same fraction of a whole.

Are $\frac{2}{4}$ and $\frac{4}{8}$ equivalent fractions? (Yes)

Compare the numerator and denominator of $\frac{2}{4}$ and $\frac{4}{8}$. Each is two times as much.

What is another equivalent fraction of $\frac{4}{8}$? ($\frac{1}{2}$)

What can we do to $\frac{1}{2}$ to get $\frac{4}{8}$? Multiply the numerator and denominator by 4. When the number of total parts is multiplied by 4, the number of shaded parts are also multiplied by 4.
Color another fourth in the strip divided into fourths.

What fraction of the strip is colored? ($\frac{3}{4}$)

Draw lines to divide each shaded part into two.

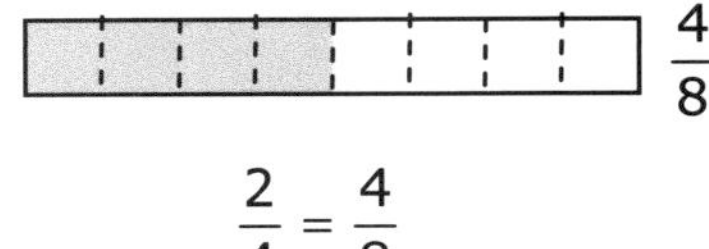

$$\frac{2}{4} = \frac{4}{8}$$

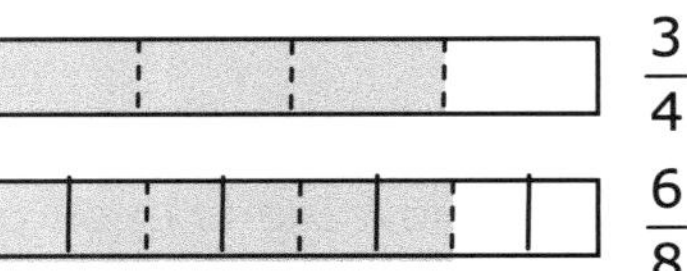

We now have 6 shaded parts. To write this as a
fraction of the whole, all the parts need to be equal,
so we also need to divide the rest of the parts into
two. How many total parts do we have? (8)

Are $\dfrac{3}{4}$ and $\dfrac{6}{8}$ equivalent fractions? (Yes)

When the number of shaded parts is multiplied by
2, the number of total parts is also multiplied by 2
so that all the parts are the same size.

We can find equivalent fractions by multiplying the numerator and denominator
by the same number.

➤ Use the fractions strip page in the appendix. Have your student look at it and
find equivalent fractions. Help him determine the number by which the
numerator and denominator needs to be multiplied to get the equivalent
fraction.

Learning Tasks 1-3, 3d➤pp 58-59 US➤pp. 71-72

In learning task 1, note that the original parts are being divided up into smaller
parts. In (a) each part is divided into two parts. The total number of parts is
multiplied by 2, so to get an equivalent fraction, the number of shaded parts is
multiplied by 2. (Each part is half as big.)
In 2(a), the whole is being divided into 2 parts, 3 parts, or 8 parts.
In 2(b), the third is being divided into 2 parts, 3 parts, or 4 parts.
In 3, guide the student to first find the number by which the denominator or
numerator is being multiplied. For example, in (a) ask 4 x what = 12? (3). So
multiply 1 by 3. Use fraction strips to illustrate, if necessary.

1.　(a) 4　　　　(b) 6　　　　(c) 8
　　(d) $\dfrac{10}{15}$, $\dfrac{12}{18}$, $\dfrac{14}{21}$

2.　(a) 2; 3; $\dfrac{8}{8}$　(b) 2; 9; $\dfrac{4}{12}$

3.　(a) 3　　　　(b) 6　　　　(c) 2
　　(d) 18　　　(e) 10　　　(f) 8

Workbook Exercises 31 and 32

In exercise 32, #3, the pair $\dfrac{2}{6}$ and $\dfrac{3}{9}$ may not be obvious to your student. Use
fraction strips to show they are equivalent for now.

(2) Equivalent Fractions by Division

 Find an equivalent fraction by dividing the numerator and denominator by a constant.

 Your student should be able to easily see when two numbers between 1 and 12 can be divided by the same number. You can review this with games, if desired.

Material: Four or more sets of **number cards** 1-12, **dice**.

Procedure: Shuffle the cards. Turn over five cards and place them face up. The players take turns throwing the die and getting as many multiples of the number on the die as possible. For example, there are cards for 1, 5, 6, 8 and 12 in the center. The player throws a 4. He can remove the cards 8 and 12. Note that if he throws a 1, he gets all the cards in the center. After each turn, replace the cards that have been removed with more cards from the stack. The player with the most cards at the end wins.

Material: Four sets of **number cards**, 2-12.

Procedure: Shuffle the cards. Turn over two and lay them down next to each other in a line. If they can be divided by the same number, other than 1, remove them from the line, and turn over two more cards. If they cannot be divided by the same number, turn over one card at a time, adding them to the line, until two next to each other can be removed.

 Use two fraction strips or circles, or draw bars, one showing thirds and one showing sixths. Place the one showing sixths above the one showing thirds.

What is the total number of parts in the first bar?

(6) Each part is what fraction? ($\frac{1}{6}$)

What is the total number of parts in the second bar? (3)

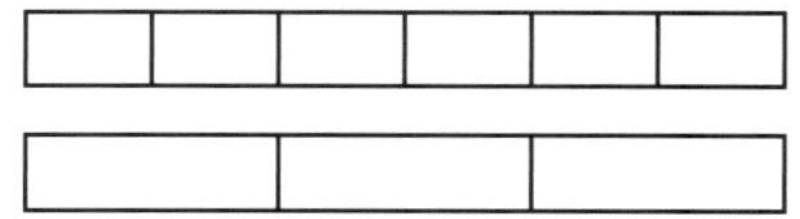

We divided the total number of parts by 2.
Each part in the second bar is how much bigger than in the first bar (Twice as big.)

Shade $\frac{4}{6}$ on the first bar. How much would you shade on the second bar to get an equivalent fraction? (2 parts.)

What is the equivalent fraction? ($\frac{2}{3}$)

When the total number of parts is divided by 2, the total number of shaded parts is also divided by 2.

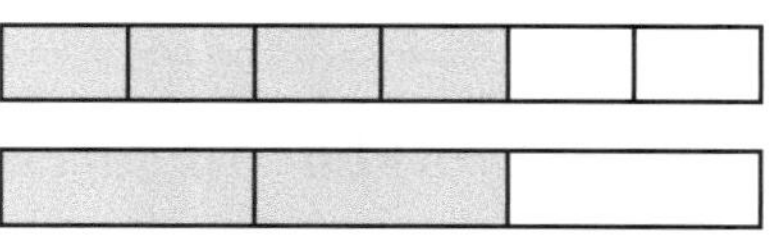

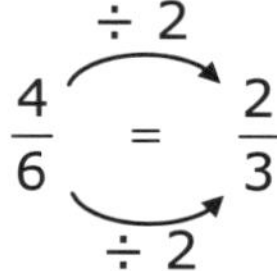

Draw a bar and show $\frac{6}{9}$. Combine parts to find an

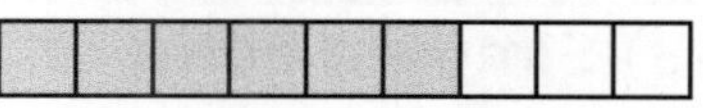

equivalent fraction for $\frac{6}{9}$. ($\frac{2}{3}$) The shaded part

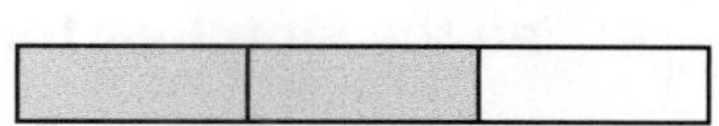

was divided by how much? (3) The whole bar was divided by how much? (3).

When the total number of shaded parts is divided by 3, the total number of parts is also divided by 3.

$$\frac{6}{9} \overset{\div 3}{\underset{\div 3}{=}} \frac{2}{3}$$

We can find equivalent fractions by dividing the numerator and denominator by the same number.

➤ **Optional:**

Use the fraction strips to see if you can find another fraction equivalent to $\frac{6}{9}$ with a denominator of 6.

$$\frac{6}{9} = \frac{}{6}$$
$$\frac{6}{9} = \frac{4}{6}$$

We cannot find every equivalent fraction by multiplying or dividing the numerator by a simple number.

List some equivalent fractions of $\frac{6}{9}$. First multiply the numerator and denominator by 2, then 3, then 4.

$$\frac{6}{9},\ \frac{12}{18},\ \frac{18}{27},\ \frac{24}{36}$$

List some equivalent fractions of $\frac{4}{6}$.

$$\frac{4}{6},\ \frac{8}{12},\ \frac{12}{18},\ \frac{16}{24}$$

What do you notice? $\frac{12}{18}$ is an equivalent fraction for both.

To find $\frac{6}{9} = \frac{}{6}$, you can list the equivalent fractions of $\frac{6}{9}$ until you get one where there is a denominator that you can divide by some number to get 6. What is the denominator? (18) What number can you divide this by to get 6? (3). Divide the numerator by the same number, and you can find an equivalent fraction of $\frac{6}{9}$ with a denominator of 6.

 **Learning Tasks 4-5, US➤p. 73 3d➤p. 60**

4.   4; 3   4; 3

5.   (a) 4   (b) 1   (c) 2
      (d) 3   (e) 4   (f) 6

 **Workbook Exercise 33**

(3) Simplest Form

 Find the **simplest form** of a fraction.

When we divide the numerator and denominator of a fraction to get an equivalent fraction, we are simplifying it. If the numerator and denominator cannot be divided by the same number, it is in its simplest form.

 Write the fraction $\frac{8}{12}$. You can also draw a bar representing this fraction. Ask your student to find equivalent fractions by dividing the numerator and denominator by the same number.

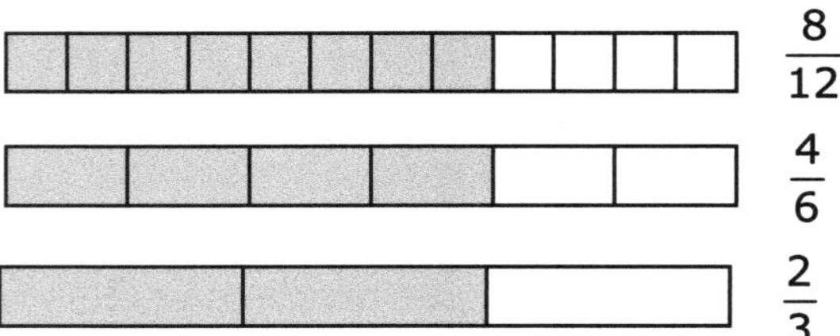

Tell him that when the numerator and denominator are divided by the same number, we are **simplifying** the fraction. We are making it simpler by finding the smallest number of parts into which the whole needs to be divided. The **simplest fraction** is the one where we cannot divide the numerator and denominator by the same number. We have simplified it as far as we can. This fraction is called the **simplest form** of the equivalent fractions. The simplest form of $\frac{8}{12}$ is $\frac{2}{3}$.

 **Learning Tasks 6-7, US▶pp. 73-74 3d▶pp. 60-61**
In learning task 7, point out that we can use more than one step to find the simplest form. For example, with (e), she can notice first that $\frac{4}{12}$ can be simplified as $\frac{2}{6}$, and then as $\frac{1}{3}$. If she finds the biggest number by which both the numerator and denominator can be divided, she can do it in one step, but sometimes it is easier to do it in several steps. She should always look at her simpler fraction to make sure that it cannot be further simplified.

6.   6   4   2 $\frac{1}{2}$

7.   (a) $\frac{1}{2}$ (b) $\frac{3}{4}$ (c) $\frac{1}{2}$ (d) $\frac{1}{3}$

     (e) $\frac{1}{3}$ (f) $\frac{2}{3}$ (g) $\frac{5}{6}$ (h) $\frac{3}{5}$

 **Workbook Exercise 34**

(4) Comparing Fractions US➤(p. 74) 3d➤(p. 61)

 Compare and order fractions.

 **Learning Tasks 8-9, US➤ p. 74 3d➤ p. 61**

Copy and cut out fraction circles from the appendix, or draw some so that your student can write on them, or use fraction bars. Color them as in the text.

Ask your student to tell you which fraction is greater. The answer is obvious from looking at the fraction circle pictures. Tell him that in order to compare fractions when he doesn't have a picture to look at he needs to have all the parts the same size so that he can find out whether he has more parts. Have him divide each of the parts in the fraction circle representing fourths in half. Ask him for the equivalent fraction.

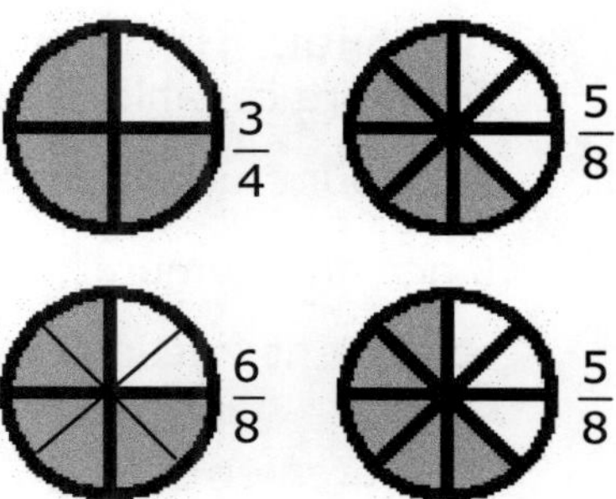

Remind him that he has already learned how to compare fractions where the numerators or the denominators are the same. If the numerators are the same, the greater fraction is the one with the smallest denominator. Both have the same number of pieces, but the parts are larger when the denominator is smaller.

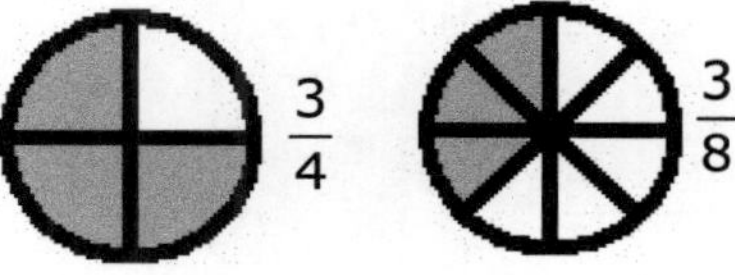

In order to compare fractions where neither the numerator nor denominator are the same, we need to find equivalent fractions where they are the same so that we can compare them. Usually we find equivalent fractions where the denominator is the same.

➤ For learning task 9, point out that the denominator in $\frac{7}{10}$ is twice the denominator in $\frac{2}{5}$, so we can find an equivalent fraction for $\frac{2}{5}$ where the denominator is 10. Have your student supply the equivalent fraction $\frac{4}{10}$ and tell you which is greater, $\frac{4}{10}$ or $\frac{7}{10}$.

➤ For most of the problems in this section, in which fractions are compared or ordered, the fractions are related, that is, the denominator of one is a simple multiple of the denominator of the other. In instances where they are not, as in learning tasks 10.(e) and 11.(e) in the text, allow less capable students to use fraction strips to compare them. Unrelated fractions, where one denominator is not a simple multiple of the other, will be dealt with more in *Primary Mathematics 5A*.

➤ **Optional:**
For more capable students, you can teach the following:

Ask your student which is greater, $\frac{1}{3}$ or $\frac{2}{5}$.

Since one numerator is twice the other, we could compare them by finding an equivalent fraction of $\frac{1}{3}$ where the numerator is 2. $\frac{1}{3} = \frac{2}{6}$

$\frac{2}{5}$ is greater than $\frac{2}{6}$, so $\frac{2}{5}$ is greater than the fraction $\frac{1}{3}$.

We can also list equivalent fractions for each until we get some with the same denominator.

$$\frac{2}{5},\ \frac{4}{10},\ \left(\frac{6}{15}\right)$$

$$\frac{1}{3},\ \frac{2}{6},\ \frac{3}{9},\ \frac{4}{12},\ \left(\frac{5}{15}\right) \qquad \frac{6}{15} \text{ is greater than } \frac{5}{15}, \text{ so } \frac{2}{5} \text{ is greater than } \frac{1}{3}.$$

Have your student look at the lists to see if he can see a pattern.

$\dfrac{2}{5},\ \dfrac{4}{10},\ \dfrac{6}{15}$ The numerator increases by 2 while the denominator increases by 5

$\dfrac{1}{3},\ \dfrac{2}{6},\ \dfrac{3}{9},\ \dfrac{4}{12},\ \dfrac{5}{15}$ The numerator increases by 1 while the denominator increases by 3.

Ask him whether he thinks it is easier to start with the fraction with the greater or smaller denominator.

If he starts with the fraction with the greater denominator, he can list equivalent fractions until he gets one with a denominator that can be divided by the denominator of the other fraction. and then find an equivalent fraction with that denominator. $\frac{6}{15}$ has a denominator that can be divided by 3, determine the numerator for $\frac{1}{3} = \frac{}{15}$. If he started with the fraction with the smaller denominator he would have to list more fractions until he found one with a denominator he can divide by 5.

➤ At this level, fractions are ordered by listing when one denominator is not a multiple of the other. Although it is not taught here, you may also want to point out to your student that he can find equivalent fractions by multiplying the numerator and denominator of one fraction by the denominator of the other fraction:

To compare $\frac{1}{3}$ and $\frac{2}{5}$, multiply the numerator and denominator of $\frac{1}{3}$ by 5, the denominator of $\frac{2}{5}$, and multiply the numerator and denominator of $\frac{2}{5}$ by 3, the denominator of $\frac{1}{3}$:

$$\frac{1}{3} = \frac{5}{15} \quad (\times 5) \qquad\qquad \frac{2}{5} = \frac{6}{15} \quad (\times 3)$$

➤ Write the following fractions and ask your student if each of them is greater than or less than $\frac{1}{2}$, and why:

$\frac{3}{8}$ — less - $\frac{4}{8}$ is equivalent to $\frac{1}{2}$, and $\frac{3}{8}$ is less than $\frac{4}{8}$. 3 is less than half of 8.

$\frac{5}{6}$ — more - $\frac{3}{6}$ is equivalent to $\frac{1}{2}$; $\frac{5}{6}$ is more than $\frac{3}{6}$. 5 is more than half of 6.

$\frac{7}{12}$ — more – 7 is more than half of 12.

$\frac{4}{10}$ — less – 4 is less than half of 10.

$\frac{5}{7}$ — more - 7 cannot be divided in half, but $6 \div 2$ is 3, $7 \div 2$ is 3 r1, and $8 \div 2$ is 4. So $7 \div 2$ is between 3 and 4.

$\frac{2}{5}$ — less - 2 is less than half of 5.

Now, Ask your student to arrange the fractions $\frac{7}{9}$, $\frac{1}{4}$, $\frac{5}{6}$ and $\frac{3}{8}$ from smallest to greatest. The first step is to compare the fractions with $\frac{1}{2}$.

$\frac{1}{4}$ and $\frac{3}{8}$ are less than $\frac{1}{2}$.

$\frac{7}{9}$ and $\frac{5}{6}$ are greater than $\frac{1}{2}$.

Compare $\frac{1}{4}$ and $\frac{3}{8}$. $\frac{1}{4} = \frac{2}{8}$, $\frac{1}{4}$ is less than $\frac{3}{8}$.

Compare $\frac{7}{9}$ and $\frac{5}{6}$ by listing until you come to the same denominator.

$\frac{7}{9}, \left(\frac{14}{18}\right)$

$\frac{5}{6}, \frac{10}{12}, \left(\frac{15}{18}\right)$ $\frac{7}{9}$ is smaller than $\frac{5}{6}$.

The order is $\frac{1}{4}$, $\frac{3}{8}$, $\frac{7}{9}$, $\frac{5}{6}$

 **Learning Tasks 10-12, US▶p. 74 3d▶p. 61**

10. (a) $\frac{5}{6}$ (b) $\frac{1}{2}$ (c) $\frac{3}{5}$

11. (a) $\frac{7}{10}$ (b) $\frac{5}{6}$ (c) $\frac{3}{5}$

12. (a) $\frac{1}{2}$, $\frac{5}{8}$, $\frac{3}{4}$ (b) $\frac{3}{10}$, $\frac{2}{5}$, $\frac{3}{5}$

 **Workbook Exercise 35**

Practice

 **Practice 6B, US▸p. 75 3d▸p. 62**

1. (a) 2   (b) 9   (c) 2, 3
   (d) 2   (e) 2   (f) 2, 3

2. (a) 10   (b) 12   (c) 6, 9
   (d) 2   (e) 4   (f) 6, 10

3. (a) $\dfrac{7}{10}$ (b) $\dfrac{5}{6}$ (c) $\dfrac{10}{12}$

   (d) $\dfrac{5}{6}$ (e) $\dfrac{3}{4}$ (f) $\dfrac{5}{8}$

4. (a) $\dfrac{1}{7}$, $\dfrac{3}{7}$, $\dfrac{5}{7}$ (b) $\dfrac{1}{10}$, $\dfrac{1}{5}$, $\dfrac{1}{2}$

   (c) $\dfrac{1}{2}$, $\dfrac{2}{3}$, $\dfrac{5}{6}$ (d) $\dfrac{1}{4}$, $\dfrac{5}{12}$, $\dfrac{2}{3}$

3d▸ 5. Suchen
US▸ 5. Sara

Review

 **Review D, US▸pp. 76-77 3d▸p. 63-64**

1. (a) 9210   (b) 4060

2. (a) six thousand, two hundred four
    (b) three thousand, five hundred forty
    (c) five thousand twenty-eight

3. 3900

4. (a) 4014, 4041, 4104, 4410   (b) 1112, 2111, 2121, 2211

5. 1000

6. 62 r4

7. 11

8. (a) 20   (b) 30

9. (a) 3   (b) 9   (c) 5

10. (a) $\dfrac{1}{4}$ (b) $\dfrac{2}{7}$ (c) $\dfrac{11}{12}$

    (d) $\dfrac{3}{6}$ (e) $\dfrac{3}{8}$ (f) $\dfrac{2}{5}$

11. (a) 420 cm   (b) 2 m 5 cm
    (c) 2095 m   (d) 1 km 600 m
    (e) 1040 g   (f) 2 kg 450 g
    (g) 3060 ml   (h) 2ℓ 525 ml

12. Cost of 6 pears = 6 x 70 = 420 = \$4.20
    Change = \$5 - \$4.20 = **80¢**

13. Amount more = \$38.40 - \$9.60 = **\$28.80**

14. Amount left = 1ℓ − 325 ml = **675 ml**

15. Total milk = 10 x 125 ml = 1250 ml = **1ℓ 250 ml**

16. Fraction saved = $1 - \dfrac{4}{9} = \dfrac{\mathbf{5}}{\mathbf{9}}$

17. Fraction spent on racket = $1 - \dfrac{3}{7} = \dfrac{\mathbf{4}}{\mathbf{7}}$

 **Workbook Review 4**
Workbook Review 6

Unit 7 Time

Part 1 Hours and Minutes

---

(1) Telling Time and Duration

- ➢ Tell time from a clock face.
- ➢ Understand a.m. and p.m.
- ➢ Find the duration of a time interval of hours or minutes.

In *Primary Mathematics 2*, students learned how to tell time to five minute intervals and to determine time intervals within 60 minutes or over several hours. This is reviewed in this section, and extended to telling time to the one minute interval.

Though analog clocks are becoming rarer, when looking at them we often estimate the time to the nearest five minutes. With an analog clock, rather than a digital clock, it is easy to see how much time there is left for the hour, half-hour, or quarter hour to be up. We can just look at how far around the minute hand needs to go. People who are used to analog, or face clocks, often imagine the hands on the clock face in their minds when looking at the time on a digital clock, and think in terms of how far the minute hand has moved around the circle. People who are more used to digital clocks will think of time more in terms of 60 minutes and fractions of 60.

➤ Use a real **clock** or a demonstration one with geared hands that show the relationship between the minute hand and the hour hand.

Remind your student that there are 60 minutes in an hour. Set the time on the clock and ask her to tell you the time and write the digital time. Discuss different ways of saying the time. For example, set the clock at 10:45. She writes 10:45. This could be called:

> Ten forty-five
> Forty-five minutes after 10 o'clock
> Fifteen minutes to 11 o'clock
> A quarter to 11

Give some times, phrased in different ways, and have your student show the time on the clock.

➤ Set the time on the demonstration clock to various times between the five-minute marks and have your student first estimate the time to the nearest five minutes, and then give the actual time.

➤ Remind your student that a.m. (ante-meridiem) means before noon, and p.m. (post-meridiem) means after noon. Meridian is when the sun is at its highest point in the sky. Remind her that there are 24 hours in a day. 0 hours is midnight, 1 is one hour after midnight, 12 is 12 hours after midnight, and is in the middle of the day, or noon. The next hour is 1 o'clock again, but means one hour after noon, rather than one hour after midnight, so we use p.m. to show which 12 hour period we mean. Sometimes time is given according to a 24 hour clock, as in the military. 1:00 p.m. would then be 13:00. Have your student practice converting between 12-hour time and 24-hour time.

Page US▸78 3d▸65
Learning Tasks 1-5, US▸pp. 79-81 3d▸pp. 66-68
This is primarily review. Provide other examples using a real clock or demonstration clock, if necessary. In learning task 3, your student can use his finger to point to the 5 minute marks and count by 5's to 20 from 9:30 and then by 1's to 26 to show that he will end up at 9:56. He can also add 26 to 30. In learning task 5.(c) he must first think of the hour hand as moving 2 hours to get to 11:15, or the minute hand going around two full times, and then the minute hand moving another 15 minutes to 11:30.

2.   (a) 2:05   (b) 4:15   (c) 12:20   (d) 7:30
      (e) 3:40   (f) 7:45

3.   9:56

4.   60 minutes

5.   (a) 27   (b) 5   (c) 2 h 15 min

➤ Show your student how he can relate learning task 5.(c) to a time line. Draw a line and mark 9:15 on it. At regular intervals, mark 10:15 and then 11:15. The next interval would be 12:15, which is past the end time of 11:30, so we stop at 11:15. We then go another 15 minutes along the time line to get to 11:30.

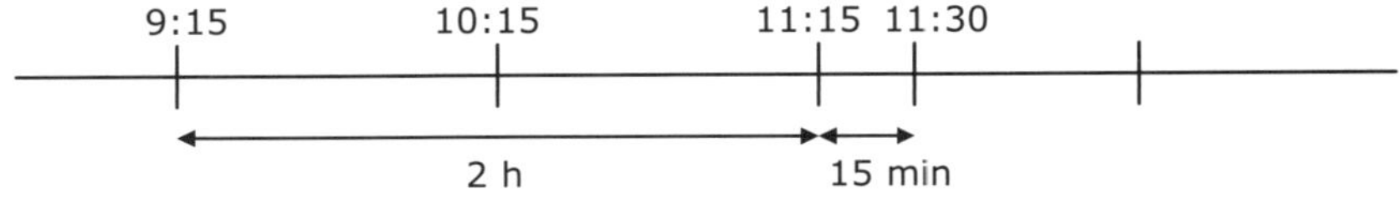

➤ Do some additional problems, using the clock, where the time goes from a.m. to p.m. or from p.m. to a.m. For example,

How long is it from 10:30 a.m. to 2:17 p.m?

Let your student use a clock to find the answer, then show how to do it on a time line:

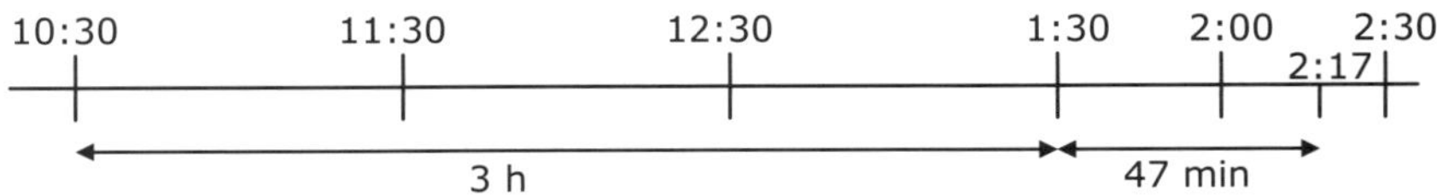

 **Workbook Exercises 36-37**

(2) Converting Between Hours and Minutes

 ➢ Convert hours and minutes to minutes, and minutes to hours and minutes.

 The origin of our minute and second goes back to the Babylonians. The Babylonians did their astronomical calculations in the sexagesimal, or base-60 system. In the base-60 system, one place value can hold 59 units. When another unit is added, the 60 units are regrouped to the next place value. So each place value is 60 times the next lower place value, or each place value is one sixtieth of the next higher place value. The Babylonians divided the hour up into base 60 fractions. The first fractional sexagesimal place (one sixtieth of one whole) we now call a **minute**; the second place, a **second**.

➤ Ask your student how many minutes are in 1 hour. 2 hours? 3 hours?

$$
\begin{aligned}
1 \text{ hour} &\rightarrow 60 \text{ minutes} \\
2 \text{ hours} &\rightarrow 120 \text{ minutes} \\
3 \text{ hours} &\rightarrow 180 \text{ minutes} \\
4 \text{ hours} &\rightarrow 240 \text{ minutes} \\
5 \text{ hours} &\rightarrow 300 \text{ minutes} \\
6 \text{ hours} &\rightarrow 360 \text{ minutes} \\
7 \text{ hours} &\rightarrow 420 \text{ minutes} \\
8 \text{ hours} &\rightarrow 480 \text{ minutes} \\
9 \text{ hours} &\rightarrow 540 \text{ minutes} \\
10 \text{ hours} &\rightarrow 600 \text{ minutes}
\end{aligned}
$$

Practice counting by 60 up to 10 x 60.

➤ Ask your student how many hours are in 60 minutes. 180 minutes? Continue to ask for the number of hours in multiples of 60 minutes.

Ask your student for the number of minutes in 4 h 40 minutes. He must first determine the number of minutes in 4 hours by multiplying 4 by 60, and then add the product to 40.

4 h 40 min = 240 min + 40 min = 280 min

Do other examples if necessary.

Ask your student for the number of minutes in 220 minutes. He must first think of the multiple of 60 that is closest to 220 without being more than 220. This will give the number of hours. He then subtracts this from 220 to get the number of minutes.

220 min = 180 min + 40 min = 3 h 40 min

 **Learning Tasks 6-10, US>p. 82 3d>p. 69**

6.   (a) Jane   (b) **US>** Amy   **3d>** Aihua

7.   95

8.   (a) 120 min (b) 130 min (c) 165 min
     (d) 180 min (e) 185 min (f) 195 min

9.   3 h 20 min

10. (a) 1 h 10 min   (b) 1 h 25 min   (c) 1 h 40 min
     (d) 2 h 5 min   (e) 2 h 40 min   (f) 3 h 30 min

 **Workbook Exercise 38**

(3) Time Intervals

> ➢ Find the duration of a time interval using a time line.
> ➢ Find the start time given the end time and the duration using a time line.
> ➢ Find the end time given the start time and the duration using a time line.

Practice making 60. Give your student a number between 0 and 60 and ask how much more is needed to make 60 minutes, or 1 hour. Do mostly multiples of 5, but include others.

Write down two times, such as 10:30 and 11:15, with a time interval of less than 60, and ask your student for the number of minutes between those times. Show her a time line for this. She can count up to the hour (60 minutes) and then add on the rest of the minutes.

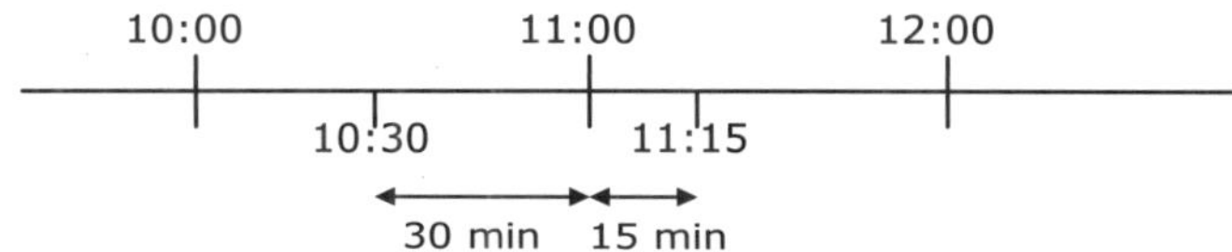

Do the same with times for more than an hour. For example, write down 3:40 and 6:20. Use a time line to show how she can count by hours first (4:40, 5:40) then by minutes to the next hour (20 minutes from 5:40 to 6:00) and by minutes after the hour (20 minutes from 6:00 to 6:20). The total duration is 2 hours 40 minutes.

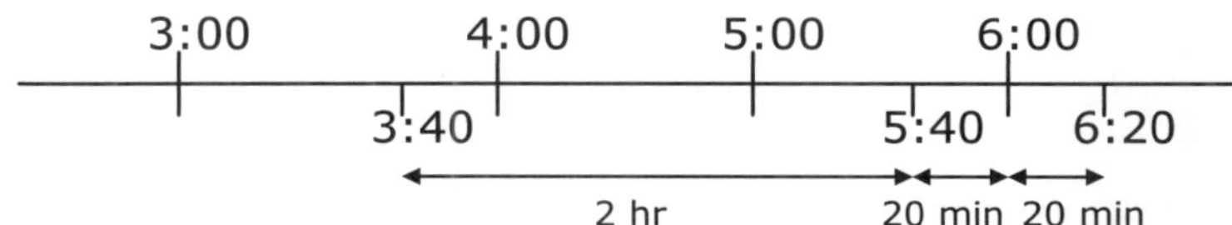

Now ask her how long it is between two times that involve a change from a.m. to p.m. or from p.m. to a.m. For example, write down 10:30 a.m. and 2:05 p.m. We can count first by hours to 12:30, then switch over for the next hour to 1:30, then by minutes to 2:05. It is 3 hours and 35 minutes from 10:30 a.m. to 2:05 p.m.

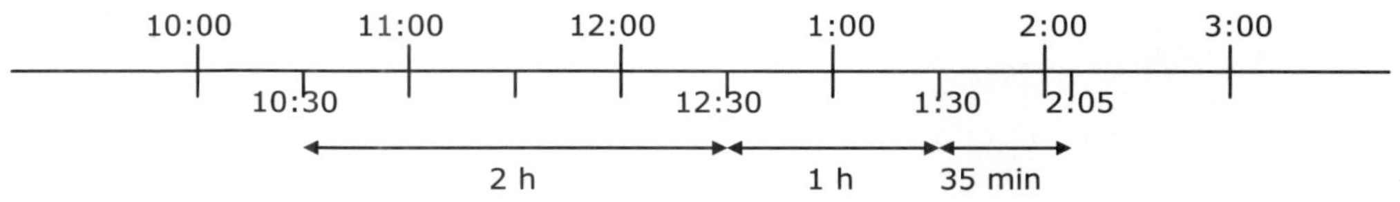

Do other examples as necessary.

 **Learning Tasks 11-13, US➤p. 83 3d➤p. 70**
Draw a time line, if necessary, to help your student solve these problems.

11. 1 h 5 min

12. 9:00 a.m.
     One hour later than 7:15 a.m. is 8:15 a.m., another 45 min brings the
     minute hand around to the hour, or 9:00 a.m.

13. 8:30 p.m.
     One hour sooner than 9:40 p.m. is 8:40 p.m., another 10 min earlier is
     8:30

 **Workbook Exercise 39**

(4) Adding and Subtracting Hours and Minutes

- Add and subtract time (hours and minutes) in compound units.
- Find the duration of a time interval by adding or subtracting hours and minutes.
- Find the end time given the start time and the duration by adding or subtracting hours and minutes.

Learning Tasks 14-15, US>p. 84 3d>p. 71

Use the examples from the learning tasks to discuss various methods for adding and subtracting hours and minutes. Do additional examples if necessary.

14. (a) 2 h   (b) 3 h 30 min   (c) 1 h 15 min

We can find the amount of time between two times, one before 12:00 and one after 12:00, as in learning task 15, in two steps:

First, we find the amount of time from the start time to 12:00.

We can do this by counting up the time: 10:15 to 11:15 is 1 hour; 11:15 to 12:00 is another 45 minutes; the total time is 1 h 45 min.

Next, we add that to the end time, since the end time is the amount of time after 12:00.

To add the times, we first add the hours, then the minutes. If the minutes are more than 60, we have to rename 60 of them as an hour. We can do that in two ways:

Add the minutes, then rename 60 minutes as 1 hour and add 1 hour to the hours:

$$10 \text{ h } 45 \text{ min} + 30 \text{ min} = 10 \text{ h } 75 \text{ min} = 11 \text{ h } 15 \text{ min}$$

60 min   15 min

Or, make 60:

$$10 \text{ h } 45 \text{ min} + 30 \text{ min} = 11 \text{ h } 15 \text{ min}$$

15 min   15 min

60 min

11 h

 You may want to tell your student that we can also convert to 24 hours by adding 12 to the hours for the final time, thinking of both times as hours and minutes, and subtracting. To find the time between 10:15 a.m. and 9:30 p.m.:

10:15 a.m. → 10 h 15 min
9:30 p.m. → 9 h + 12 h + 30 min = 21 h 30 min
21 h 30 min – 10 h 15 min = 11 h 45 min

To find the time between 10:45 p.m. and 7:30 a.m.:

10:45 p.m. → 10 h 45 min
7:30 a.m. → 7 h + 12 h + 30 min = 19 h 30 min

Subtract the hours, then subtract 45 minutes from one of the hours and add the difference to 30 minutes:

19 h 30 min – 10 h 45 min = 9 h 30 min – 45 min = 8 h 45 min

8 h   1 h

15 min

Learning Tasks 16-17, US▸p. 85 3d▸p. 72

16.   (a) 4 h   (b) 6 h 40 min   (c) 2 h 50 min

We can find the end time when the end time will be past 12:00, as in learning task 17, in two main steps:

First, we find the amount of time from the start time to 12:00.

We can do this by counting up the time to 12:00: 10:30 to 11:30 is 1 hour, 11:30 to 12:00 is another 30 minutes; the total time is 1 h 30 min.

Next, we subtract the time to 12:00 from the total time.

To do this, we subtract the hours first.

3 h 20 min – 1 h 30 min = 2 h 20 min – 30 min.

Then we subtract the minutes. Here there are not enough minutes from which to subtract from, so we rename an hour as 60 minutes:

2 h 20 min – 30 min = 1 h 80 min – 30 min = 1 h 50 min

Or, we can subtract from the hour:

$$2 \text{ h } 20 \text{ min } - 30 \text{ min } = 1 \text{ h } 50 \text{ min}$$

1 h   1 h

30 min

> You may want to tell your student that we can also add the hours and minutes, and then convert from 24 hour time to 12 hour time if it is more than 12 hours by subtracting 12 from the hours:

10:30 p.m. → 10 h 30 min
10 h 30 min + 3 h 20 min = 13 h 50 min
13 h 50 min → 13 h − 12 h + 50 min = 1 h 50 min
1 h 50 min → 1:50 a.m.

To find the time 6 h 45 min after 9:30 a.m.:

9:30 a.m. → 9 h 30 min
9 h 30 min + 6 h 45 min = 15 h 30 min + 45 min   (add the hours)
                        = 16 h 15 min   (add the minutes)
16 h 15 min → 16 h − 12 h + 15 min = 4 h 15 min
4 h 15 min → 4:15 p.m.

Learning Task 18, US➤p. 85 3d➤p. 72

18.   (a) 5 h 40 min   (b) 3 h 5 min
      (c) 1 h 15 min   (d) 2 h 35 min
      (e) 3 h 40 min   (f) 5 h 5 min
      (g) 2 h 15 min   (h) 1 h 40 min

Workbook Exercise 40

Practice

 **Practice 7A, US>p. 86 3d>p. 73**

1. (a) 3 h 45 min   (b) 1 h 40 min
    (c) 3 h   (d) 1 h 15 min
    (e) 3 h 20 min   (f)   40 min

2. 2:25

3. (a) 7 h 15 min
    (b) 1 h 15 min
    (c) 1 h 55 min
    (d) 45 min

4. (a) 4 h 30 min
    (b) 40 min

5. 11:50 a.m.

6. 12:40 p.m.

7. 8:50 a.m.

Part 2 Other Units of Time

(1) Seconds

> Understand the magnitude of a second relative to a minute.
> Convert minutes and seconds to seconds or seconds to minutes and seconds.

 Tell your student that minutes are divided up into seconds. There are 60 seconds in a minute. The abbreviation for seconds is **s**.

 Use a **clock** with a second hand. Count to 60 seconds as the second hand goes around. Some digital clocks, or the clock on a computer, show seconds. Let your student watch the seconds count up to 60, then go back to 00 as the minutes increase by 1.

Page US▸87 3d▸74

Use a **stopwatch** and various activities such as those in learning task 1 to give your student an idea of the duration of a minute.

Learning Task 1-2, US▸pp. 87-88 3d▸pp. 74-75

Converting between minutes and seconds is done in the same way as converting between hours and minutes. In learning task 2(a), we need to find the number of seconds in 3 minutes, and then add that to 40 seconds. In learning task 2(b), we need to find a multiple of 60 closest to 150 to get the number of minutes, and then subtract the multiple from 150 to get the number of seconds. You may want to point out that this is similar to division with a remainder. The quotient is the number of minutes and the remainder is the number of seconds.

2.   (a) 220 s   (b) 2 min 30 s

 **Workbook Exercises 41-42**

(2) Years, Months, and Weeks

 ➤ Convert years and months to months and months to years and months.
➤ Convert weeks and days to days and days to weeks and days.

➤ Tell your student that years, months, weeks, and days are units of time as well. Make sure he knows the number of months in a year and days in a week.

> 1 year = 12 months
> 1 week = 7 days

➤ Ask your student how many months are in 1 year. 2 years? 3 years?

> 1 year → 12 months
> 2 years → 24 months
> 3 years → 36 months
> 4 years → 48 months
> 5 years → 60 months
> 6 years → 72 months
> 7 years → 84 months
> 8 years → 96 months
> 9 years → 108 months
> 10 years → 120 months

Review the multiplication facts for 12.

➤ Ask your student how many years are the same as 12 months. 72 months? Continue to ask for the number of years in multiples of 12 months.

➤ Show your student a **calendar**. Ask her how many weeks are in a month. He should notice that there are not a whole number of weeks in a month.

You may wish to discuss the number of days in a year and days in each month, and the significance of leap year. There are $365\frac{1}{4}$ days in a year, so every fourth year we add an extra day to February.

One easy way to determine the number of days in a month is to hold out your two fists in front of you. There are knuckles and valleys between each pair of knuckles. Assign the months in order to each knuckle and valley from left to right. If a month falls on a knuckle, it has 31 days, if it falls on a valley, it has 30 days, except for February, which has 28 days, or 29 in a leap year.

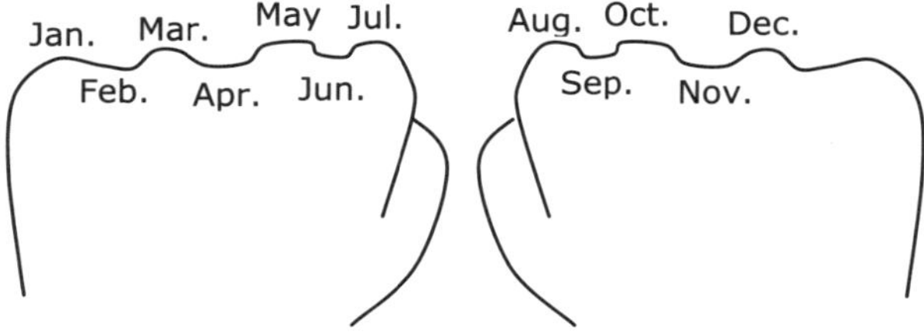

➤ Ask your student the following:

4 years 6 months = __________

> We can multiply the years by 12, then add the months.

> 4 years 6 months = 48 months + 6 months = 54 months

100 months = ________ years ________ months

> Find a multiple of 12 close to 100 years. 8 x 12 = 96. This is the number of years. The remainder is the number of months.

> 100 months = 96 months + 4 months = 8 years 4 months

5 weeks 2 days = ________ days

> Multiply the weeks by 7, then add the days.

> 5 weeks 2 days = 35 days + 2 days = 37 days

100 days = ________ weeks ________ days

> Divide by 7. The quotient is the number of weeks, and the remainder is the number of days. 100 ÷ 7 = 14 r 2

> 100 days = 14 weeks 2 days

 **Learning Tasks 3-4, US➤p. 88 3d➤p. 75**

3. (a) 12 months   (b) 24 months
    (c) 28 months   (d) 3 yrs 4 months
4. (a) 7 days   (b) 21 days
    (c) 25 days   (d) 4 weeks 2 days

 **Workbook Exercises 43 and 44**

Practice

 **Practice 7B, US➤p. 89 3d➤p. 76**

1.   (a) 132 min   (b)   1 h 48 min
     (c) 123 s   (d)   1 min 34 s
     (e) 21 months
     (f) 2 years 6 months
     (g) 19 days
     (h) 5 weeks 5 days

2.   1 h 40 min

3.   7 h 30 min

4.   2:20 p.m.

5.   56 min

6.   45 min

7.   5:30 a.m.

Review

 **Review E, US➤pp. 90-91 3d➤p. 77-78**

1. (a) 8:55 p.m.
    (b) 1:30 a.m.

2. (a) 4   (b)   8   (c) 8

3. (a) 15
    (b) Number of cars and vans = 45 + 30 = 75
         Number of spaces not occupied = 90 − 75 = **15**

US➤ 4. Mr. Lee stayed 9 months longer
3d➤ 4. Mr. Lin stayed 9 months longer

5. Number of jars in 1 min = 140 ÷ 10 = **14**

6. 6:25 p.m.

7. Capacity of bucket = 60 ℓ ÷ 10 = **6 ℓ**

8. Length of other piece = 1 m - $\dfrac{5}{8}$ m = $\dfrac{3}{8}$ m

9. Total cost = $6.50 + $1.80 = **$8.30**

10. Number of mangoes given to children = 16 x 3 = 48
    Number of mangoes in box = number remaining + number given
                             = 48 + 20
                             = **68**

11. Total cost = $4.80 + $2.50 = **$7.30**

12. (a) Cost of towels = $50 - $2 = **$48**
    (b) Cost of one towel = $48 ÷ 8 = **$6**

 **Workbook Review 7**

Unit 8 Geometry

Part 1 Angles

---

(1) Angles

➢ Identify angles.
➢ Relate the number of sides of a closed figure with straight lines to the number of angles.

In this section, students will intuitively learn the concept of an angle. They should determine that an angle is formed when two straight lines meet at a point. They should also determine a closed figure formed by straight lines has the same number of angles as sides. Measurement of angles will be taught in *Primary Mathematics 4*.

Go through the activities and learning tasks in the text with your student. For creating an angle from two cards, you can use two index cards. Make a "hinge" with tape. As your student investigates angles, relate their sizes to the amount of turning, or opening, of the hinged cards. From learning task 3 and the workbook exercise, your student should come to the conclusion that closed figures with straight lines have the same number of sides as angles.

Page US➤92 3d➤79
Learning Tasks 1-3, US➤p. 93 3d➤p. 80

a is the smallest, c is the biggest

2.   3 sides, 3 angles

3.   4

Draw two figures with equal angles but different lengths of the two arms. Draw each one with marker or dark pen on separate pieces of thin paper so that they are visible through the paper.

Ask your student if the angles are the same. She can lay them on top of each other, or she can use her cards to measure one angle, and then slide it over to compare it to the other angle. She should realize that the size of the angle is independent of the lengths of the arms.

Workbook Exercise 45

Part 2 Right Angles

(1) Right Angles

 ➢ Identify right angles and angles larger and smaller than a right angle.

 **Page US➤94 3d➤81**

 Use two strips of cardboard, about 2 cm by 10 cm, or cut a large index card in fourths lengthwise and use two strips. Line them up at right angles, punch a hole in both near the end, and fasten with a brad. When the edges are lined up, the angle formed is a right angle. If it is opened or closed more, the edges are not lined up, and the angle is larger or smaller than a right angle. Your student can use this to investigate angles in the environment by lining up the inside edge of the strips with the sides of the angle under investigation. Have her find angles that are greater than or less than a right angle. Help her relate the degree of turning to the size of the angle. The larger the angle, the more one strip has to be turned from alignment with the other strip.

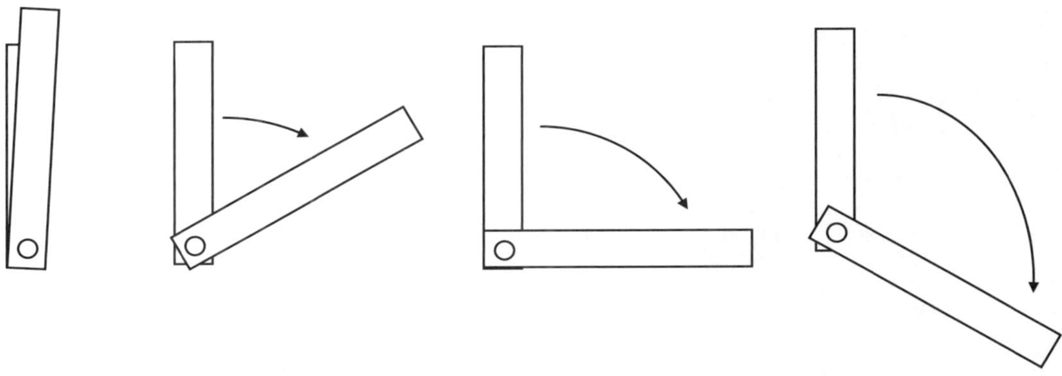

Draw a variety of angles on index cards and have your student sort them into right angles, angles smaller than a right angle (acute angles), and angles larger than a right angle (obtuse angles). Students are not required to learn the terms for acute and obtuse angles in Primary Mathematics 3, however, you may want to introduce these terms.

 Use a demonstration clock or a face clock and discuss the angles formed between the hour and minute hand at various times. For example, what is the angle formed at 9:00? At what time on the hour would another right angle be formed? Is the angle formed at 12:15 exactly a right angle, or is it a bit smaller? Are the angles formed at various times greater or smaller than a right angle?

 **Learning Tasks 1-3, US>p. 95 3d>p. 82**

1.   (a) 4   (b) 4

2.   B   C

3.   P - 4 angles, 1 right angle   Q - 5 angles, 2 right angles
     R - 4 angles, 2 right angles   S - 5 angles, 3 right angles

---

 **Workbook Exercise 46**

Enrichment 3
Möbius strip

Topology is a field of mathematics that is like geometry in that it deals with points and lines, but unlike regular geometry it allows objects to change shape and size. The Möbius strip is an interesting introduction to topology.

Make a strip of paper and tape it in such a way that it forms a circle. Mark a point on one side. Beginning at point A, draw a line the length of the strip. When you return to the point, you will have drawn a line on one side of the paper.

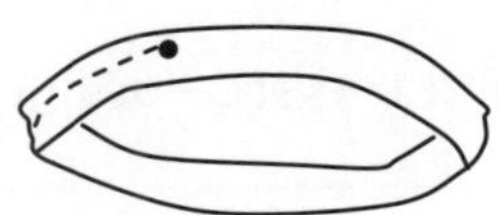

Tale another strip of paper and make a circle but put a half twist in it before taping it. This is a Möbius strip. Mark a point and draw a line along the strip. What happens? How many sides does a Möbius strip have?

Make a mark at the very edge of the strip. Run your finger along the edge of the strip. How many edges does it have?

Cut both strips in half along the lines you have drawn. What happens?

Investigate what happens if you twist the paper strip a whole turn, or a turn and a half.

After cutting the Möbius strip in half along the line, find out what happens if you cut it again along its length.

Cut a slit into both ends of a strip of paper and tape the ends together as shown. How many edges and sides does this paper have?

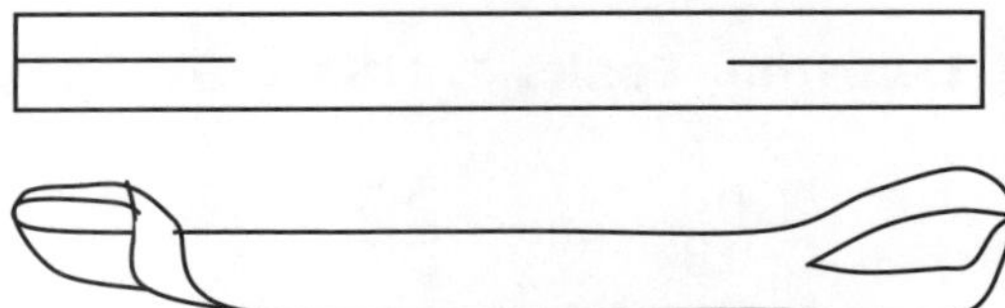

There are real-life applications of Möbius-type strips. For example, many computer printer cartridges are Möbius strips, to better utilize both sides of the ribbon. Some belts on cars and farm machinery are put together in this way, in order to provide for more uniform wear and tear on the belts.

Unit 9 Area and Perimeter

Part 1 Area

(1) Square Units

 ➢ Find the area of figures in square units.

 Students were introduced to square units in Primary Mathematics 2B. This section is a review.

 **Page US>96 3d>83**

Each figure is 6 square units. Tell your student that when a figure has an area 6 square units, that means that it can be covered up with 6 square units. The square units can be "cut up" and rearranged, as in half square units.

 Cut two units as shown and rearrange. The area of the new figure is still 2 square units.  

Cut up some other square units and rearrange. The area of each rearranged figure is the same as the original.

 **Learning Tasks 1, US>p. 97 3d>p. 84**

1.   A 6   B 5
      C 13   D 6
      E 7   F 10
      G 10   H 12
      B has the smallest area, C has the greatest area

 **Workbook Exercise 47**

(2) Units of Area

➤ Understand the relative sizes of units of area.
➤ Find the area of figures in units of area: cm^2, m^2, in.^{2}, ft^2, and yd^2.

The square centimeter and square meter are introduced in this section. For students in the US, you may also wish to discuss the relative sizes of square inches, square yards, and square feet.

Ask your student for some units of length. Possible answers are centimeter, meter, yard, inch, feet, etc.

Draw a square of side 1 cm. Tell your student that each side is 1 cm long, and the area is called 1 square centimeter. Show the abbreviation for square centimeter.

1 square centimeter: 1 cm^2

The square centimeter is a **unit of area**. We put a little two after the unit so we know that the area is equal to a square of length one cm on one side and one cm along the second side at a right angle. Two sides are 1 cm. Since it is a square, the other two sides also have to be 1 cm.

Draw a square of side 1 in. Tell your student that this is a square inch.

1 square inch: 1 in.^{2}

If we say the area of something is 4 in.^{2}, that means we can cover it up with 4 squares each an inch long on its side (even if the square needs to be cut up and rearranged).

Learning Tasks 2-5, US➤pp. 98-99 3d➤pp. 85-86

2. 4 cm^2 9 cm^2 16 cm^2

3. (a) 25 cm^2 (b) 100 cm^2

4. 10 cm^2

5. A 5 cm^2 B 8 cm^2 C 5 cm^2
D 6 cm^2 E 7 cm^2
F 6 cm^2 G 7 cm^2 H 4 cm^2

 Tape some sheets of paper together to make square feet. Make 9 of them. Show one to your student and have him measure the side. Ask him for the unit of area.

1 square foot: 1 ft^2

Arrange the 9 square feet on the floor in a 3 x 3 arrangement. Ask your student if he can give the unit of area for this figure. If necessary, remind him that there are 3 feet in a yard, so one side of the figure is one yard long.

1 square yard: 1 yd^2

Ask him how many square feet are in a square yard. Point out that even though 3 feet make a yard, this does not mean that 3 square feet make a square yard.

Use 4 meter sticks or 4 pieces of string a meter long to form a square one meter on its side, or draw a square meter on the sidewalk with chalk. Tell your student that this is another unit of measurement, a square meter.

1 square meter: 1 m^2

Put a square centimeter in the corner of the square meter. Note the relative sizes.

You may want to discuss some other units of area. In the metric system, a square kilometer is a square with 1000 meters on each side. An *are* is a square with 10 meters on each side. A *hectare* is a square with 100 meters on each side.

In U.S. standard measurement, an acre can be covered up with 4840 square yards, and a square mile can be covered up with 640 acres.

Discuss scale drawings. In a map, each square mile or square kilometer is drawn smaller so that it can fit on the map. Show your student the scale on some maps. The actual area of the land represented by the map is much bigger.

 **Learning Task 6, US➤p. 100 3d➤p. 87**
Point out that these squares are scaled down to fit on the page. A square meter is actually much bigger than that drawn here. It has been scaled down so it will fit. So it is important to pay attention to the measurements given on the page.

6.   A 6 m^2 B 4 m^2 C 5 m^2
     A has the greatest area, B has the smallest area

 **Workbook Exercises 48-49**

Part 2 Perimeter

(1) Perimeter

 ➢ Find the perimeter of a figure.

 **Page US▶101 3d▶88**

Tell your student that he can imagine the perimeter of a figure by taking its outline and opening the outline up and straightening it out to be one long line. The perimeter is the length of this line. Or he can imagine a very small person walking all around the "rim" of the figure – the perimeter is how far he has to walk.

Caution your student to be careful of corners when finding the perimeter of a rectangular figure in which the square units are shown. Some students, looking at the square on the corner, count the corner as 1 unit, rather than 2 units.

Have your student mark the starting point when counting the distance around a figure, either with her finger or with a pencil mark.

 **Learning Tasks 1-5, US▶p. 102-103 3d▶p. 89-90**

1.   Y
3.   (a) 6 cm^2 (b) A - 12 cm   B - 14 cm
4.   (a) no   (b) yes
5.   (a) Q and S   (b) R and S   (c) P and T

 Use linking cubes, square cut-outs, or centimeter graph paper to investigate the relationship of area to perimeter.

Ask your student what she could look for in figures with the same areas, such as those in learning task 5, to know if they are going to have different perimeters. Allow her to investigate by making various shapes using squares. Sides must touch along their entire length.

Any figure where a corner has squares on all four sides will have a smaller perimeter than a figure in which no corner has squares on all four sides, and the figure with most such corners has the smallest perimeter.

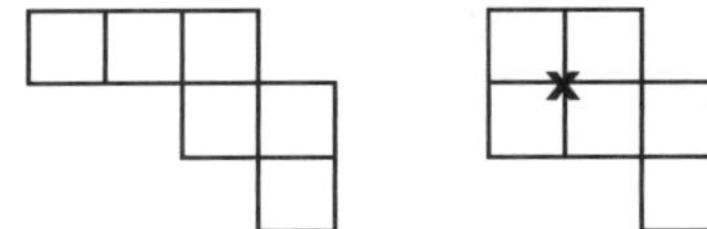

Perimeter: 14 units   12 units   10 units

➤ Have your student investigate whether the perimeter necessarily increases if the area increases.

The perimeter does not necessarily increase if the area increases.

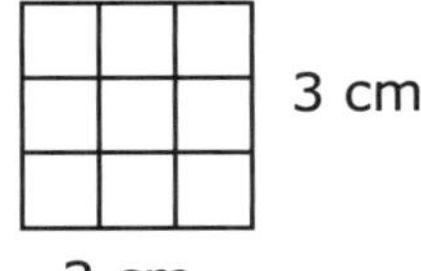   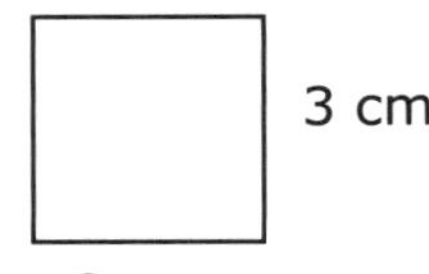

Area   5 square units   6 square units
Perimeter   12 units   10 units

➤ Use **centimeter graph paper**. Have your student draw rectangles of a given perimeter, such as 16. Have her find the area of each of the rectangles.

➤ Draw a 3 x 3 square, and label the sides 3 units long. Ask your student for the perimeter. She can count the sides of the square. Erase the inside lines and ask her if we can find the perimeter if we just know the length of the sides? The perimeter is the sum of the lengths of the sides.

Perimeter = 3 + 3 + 3 + 3 = 3 x 4 = 12 cm

In a square, since all the sides are equal, the perimeter can be found by multiplying a side by 4.

Repeat with a rectangle. Since there are two pairs of equal sides, we can add the length and the width and then multiply by two to find the perimeter.

length + width = 2 + 4 = 6 cm   Perimeter = 2 x 6 cm = 12 cm

 **Learning Tasks 6-7, US➤p. 104 3d➤p. 91**

6.   (a) 24 cm   (b) 32 cm

7.   A 25 cm   B 34 m   C 30 cm   D 39 m

 **Workbook Exercise 50**

Part 3 Area of a Rectangle

(1) Area of a Rectangle

 ➤ Find the area of a rectangle given its length and width.

 Use centimeter graph paper. Have your student draw some rectangles with an area of 24.

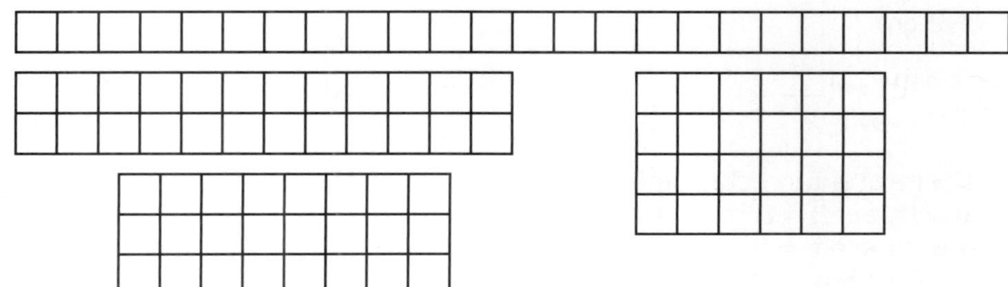

Have him write the length and width of each rectangle. Ask him if he notices anything special about the length and width. They are all numbers whose product is 24. He can find the area of a rectangle by multiplying the number of columns by the number of rows.

 **Page 3d➤92 US➤105**
Learning Tasks 1-2, US➤p. 106 3d➤p. 93

      A 8 cm^2 B 15 cm^2 C 21 cm^2 D 20 cm^2

1.   20

2.   (a) 12 cm^2 (b) 18 cm^2 (c) 24 cm^2 (d) 27 cm^2 (e) 160 cm^2

 Draw a square that has an area of 1 square foot. Draw a square inch in one corner of the figure. Ask your student for its area in square inches.

The area is 144 in.^{2}. Point out that we cannot conclude from

     1 ft = 12 inches   that   1 ft^2 = 12 in.^{2}

Since one side is 12 inches,

     1 ft^2 = 12 in. x 12 in. = 144 in.^{2}

Ask your student how many square centimeters are in a square meter.

     1 m^2 = 100 cm x 100 cm = 10,000 cm^2

 Draw the following figure and ask your student to find the total number of rectangles in this figure and the area of each.

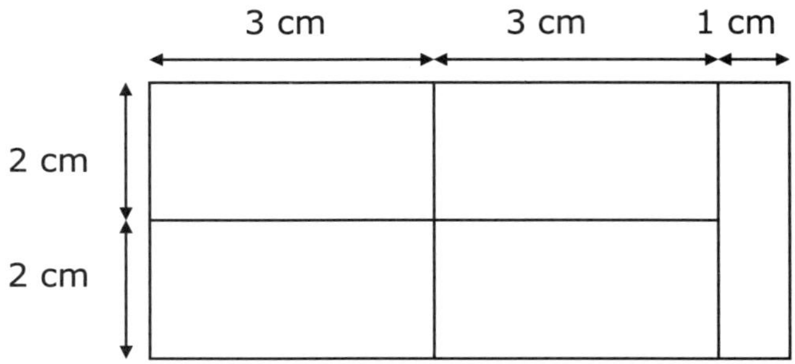

There are 11 rectangles.
1 with area =1 cm x 4 cm = 4 cm^2
4 with area = 3 cm x 2 cm = 6 cm^2
2 with area = 2 cm x 6 cm = 12 cm^2
2 with area = 3 cm x 4 cm = 12 cm^2
1 with area = 4 cm x 4 cm = 16 cm^2
1 with area = 7 cm x 4 cm = 28 cm^2

 **Workbook Exercises 51-52**

Enrichment 4
Pentominoes

Use linking cubes or centimeter graph paper.

Have your student investigate how many different shapes can be made from 4 squares. The sides must touch along their entire side – all angles must be right angles. There are only five unique shapes (different outlines resulting from flipping or rotating do not count as unique shapes). 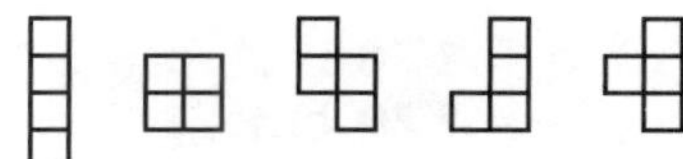

Now let your student see how many unique shapes can be made from 5 squares. There are 12.

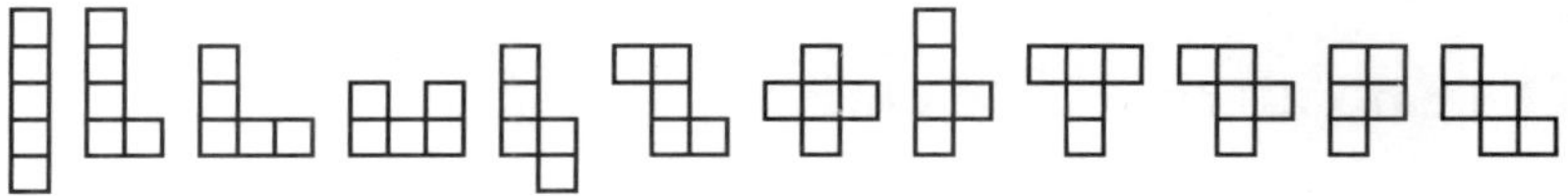

Create each shape with a different color of linking cube, or make two copies of the centimeter graph paper in the appendix, glue together back to back so that the lines line up, or to both sides of a tag board, being careful that the lines line up, and cut out each shape. These are called pentominoes.

Have your student find the perimeter of each of these pentominoes. Is there one pentomino with a perimeter different from the rest?

Have your student build rectangles from these pentominoes. This is a challenging activity. Some examples are given. What is the area of each rectangle? What is the perimeter of each rectangle? The largest rectangle uses all 12 pentominoes. There are 2,339 ways to make a rectangle using all 12 pentominoes. 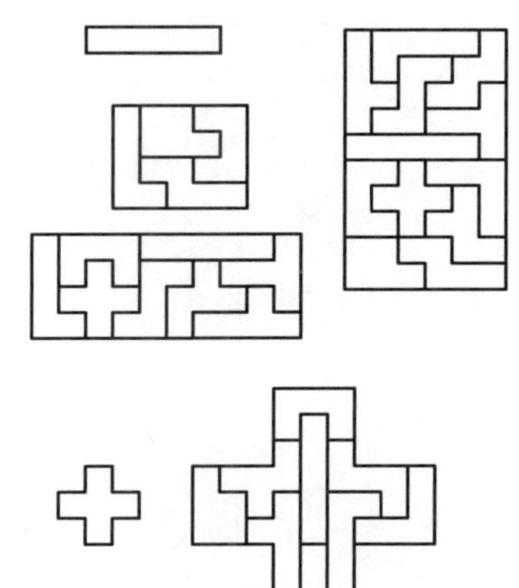

Take one of the twelve pentominoes. Use some of the others to make a copy three times as large. An example is given for one of the shapes. What is the perimeter and area of the copy?

Play a two-player strategy game. Make a game board with 8 x 8 squares of the same size as the pentominoes. Each player takes a turn placing a pentomino on the board, lining them up with the squares on the board. The last player that can arrange a piece on the board wins.

Practice

 **Practice 9A, US➤p. 107 3d➤p. 94**

1. (a) a = **25 cm²**, p = **20 cm**

US➤ (b) a = **170 in.²**, p = **54 in**
3d➤ (b) a = **170 cm²**, p = **54 cm**

(c) a = **108 cm²**, p = **48 cm**

US➤ (d) a = **64 ft²**, p = **32 ft**
3d➤ (d) a = **64 cm²**, p = **32 cm**

(e) a = **162 m²**, p = **54 m**

2. Area = 15 cm x 10 cm = **150 cm²**

3. Perimeter of field = 85 m + 10 m + 85 m + 10 m = **190 m**

Review

 **Review F, US>pp. 108-109 3d>p. 95-96**

1. (a) $\frac{1}{2}, \frac{5}{8}, \frac{3}{4}$ (b) $\frac{3}{10}, \frac{1}{2}, \frac{3}{5}$

2. Perimeter = 9 cm + 9 cm + 9 cm = **27 cm**

3. (a) 9
    (b) 14
    (c) 8

4. Length of wire = 8 x 30 cm = 240 cm = **2 m 40 cm**

5. (a) Number of adults = number of people – number of children
                = 2500 – 240
                = 2260
        Number of women = number of adults – number of men
                = 2260 – 1360 = **900**
    (b) Number more adults = number adults – number children
                = 2260 – 240 = **2020**

6. Total number of cookies sold = 286 – 30 = 256
    Number of units of 8 cookies = 256 ÷ 8 = 32
    Each unit of 8 cookies cost $1. 32 units of 8 cookies are **$32**

7. Area of square = 6 cm x 6 cm = **36 cm^2**

8. Fraction John received = $1 - \frac{2}{5} = \frac{3}{5}$

9. Distance = 1 km – 580 m = **420 m**

10. (a) 2 kg 400 g
    (b) Weight of butter = 3 x 300 g = 900 g
         Weight of flour 2 kg 400 g – 900 g = **1 kg 500 g**

11. A: area = 6 square units, perimeter = 14 units
    B: area = 7 square units, perimeter = 14 units
    C: area = 7 square units, perimeter = 16 units
    (a) B & C   (b)   A & B

Review G, US➤pp. 110-112

1. 5280

2. (a) 114 in.   (b) 70 in.   (c) 91 in.

3. (a) 6 lb 9 oz
    (b) 14 ft 1 in.
    (c) 19 qt
    (d) 5 lb 6 oz
    (e) 2 ft 10 in.
    (f) 6 gal 3 qt

4. Weight of chocolate = 1 lb 5 oz + 14 oz = 2 lb 3 oz
    Total weight = 1 lb 5 oz + 2 lb 3 oz = **3 lb 8 oz**

5. Total weight of sugar = 2 x 10 oz = 20 oz = 1 lb 4 oz
    Weight of flour = 4 lb 2 oz − 1 lb 4 oz = **2 lb 14 oz**

6. Length of table = 5 ft 6 in. = 66 in.
    Width of table = half the length = 33 in. = **2 ft 9 in.**

7. 1 pt = 2 cups
    Amount of milk still needed = 3 c − 2 c = **1 c**

8. Total gallons bought = 7 gal
    Amount left = 7 gal − 3 gal 1 qt = **3 gal 3 qt**

9. Container A has 6 cups
    Container B has 4 cups
    Container C has 7 cups
    Container D has 8 cups
    Container **D** has the most water

10. Perimeter = 11 in. + 8 in. + 6 in. + 8 in. = **33 in.**

11. Pounds bought = 72 ÷ 6 = **12 lb**

12. 2 lb 7 oz = 39 oz
    Weight of each portion = 39 oz ÷ 3 = **13 oz**

13. Weight of fruit = 25 lb 3 oz − 1 lb 4 oz = **23 lb 15 oz**
    14. 1 ft 7 in.

15. A = 37 in.
    B = 29 in.
    C = 33 in.
    D = 38 in.
    Order from longest is **D, A, C, B**

16. Area of square = 6 in. x 6 in. = **36 in.^{2}**
    Area of rectangle = 18 ft x 8 ft = **144 ft^2**

17. Total quarts = 18 x 4 = **72 quarts**

18. Length of yellow ribbon = 5 ft 4 in. − 2 ft 8 in. = 2 ft 8 in.
    Total length = 5 ft 4 in. + 2 ft 8 in. = **8 ft**

19. 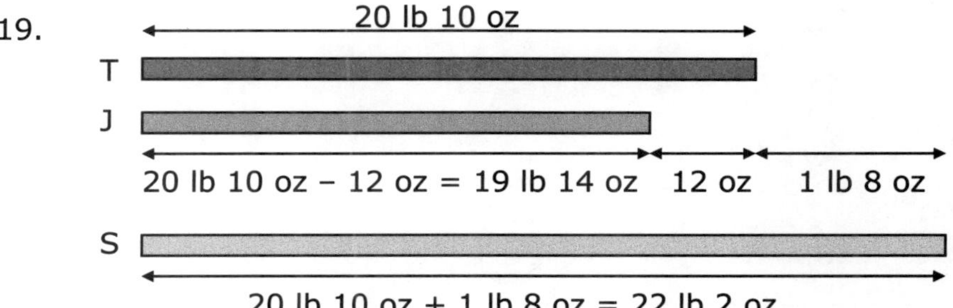

20 lb	10 oz	
19 lb	14 oz	
+ 22 lb	2 oz	
61 lb	26 oz	= **62 lb 10 oz**

The total weight is 62 lb 10 oz

20. Length and width of field = 80 ft + 50 ft = 130 ft
    Perimeter of field = 2 x 130 ft = 260 ft
    Distance run = 260 ft x 2 = **520 ft**

Workbook Review 8
Workbook Review 9

Answers to Workbook Exercises and Reviews

Exercise 1

1. (a) 92   (b) 83
   (c) 95   (d) 106

2. (a) 91   (b) 57
   (c) 98   (d) 135
   (e) 106   (f) 104

3. (a) 95, 100   (b) 114, 120

4. (a) 92   (b) 70   (c) 92   (d) 109

Exercise 2

1. (a) 92   (b) 86   (c) 130   (d) 123
   (e) 145   (f) 140   (g) 150   (h) 85

2. (a) 60   (b) 100
   (c) 70   (d) 90
   (e) 100   (f) 100
   (g) 90   (h) 100

3. (a) 105   (b) 102
   (c) 141   (d) 166
   (e) 182   (f) 135
   (g) 190   (h) 195
   (i) 197   (j) 198

Exercise 3

1. following arrows: 12, 5, 90, 27, 27, 68, 65, 38, 12

2. (a) 66, 62, 62
   (b) 47, 40, 40
   (c) 7, 2, 2

3. (a) 22   (b) 10   (c) 60   (d) 3

4. (a) 22   (b) 13   (c) 41   (d) 42

Exercise 4

1. (a) 12, 120   (b) 15, 150   (c) 20, 200   (d) 35, 350   (e) 24, 2400

2. 16   160   1600
   21   210   2100
   24   240   2400
   40   400   4000
   36   360   3600
   56   560   5600

3. (a) 12, 120   (b) 8, 800
   (c) 400   (d) 120
   (e) 140   (f) 320
   (g) 200   (h) 810
   (i) 180   (j) 140
   (k) 2400   (l) 4800
   (m) 3600   (n) 3000
   (o) 2800   (p) 600
   (q) 1800   (r) 3500

Exercise 5

1. (a) 4, 40   (b) 3, 30   (c) 2, 20   (d) 3, 300   (e) 4, 400

2. 3   30   300
   4   40   400
   5   50   500
   3   30   300
   4   40   400
   3   30   300

3. (a) 5, 50   (b) 5, 500
   (c) 20   (d) 80
   (e) 90   (f) 50
   (g) 60   (h) 80
   (i) 50   (j) 70
   (k) 900   (l) 800
   (m) 500   (n) 700
   (o) 500   (p) 600
   (q) 900   (r) 400

Exercise 6

1. (a) 47   (b) 15   (c) 26
   (d) 22   (e) 3   (f) 38

2. Answer will vary.

3. (a) 200   (b) 300
   (c) 500   (d) 900

4. (a) 4   (b) 6
   (c) 7   (d) 8

5. (a) 150   (b) 328   (c) 509

6. (a) 2 m 10 cm
   (b) 2 m 75 cm
   (c) 3 m 6 cm

7. (a) shorter than
   (b) equal to
   (c) longer than

8. (a) 10   (b) 35   (c) 95   (d) 70

Exercise 7

1. (a) 3 m 85 cm   (b) 4 m 70 cm   (c) 6 m 10 cm

2. (a) 4 m 20 cm   (b) 5 m 85 cm   (c) 7 m 68 cm
   (d) 4 m 26 cm   (e) 7 m 18 cm

3. (a) 1 m 10 cm   (b) 2 m 59 cm   (c) 6 m 39 cm

4. (a) 1 m 89 cm   (b) 4 m 12 cm
   (c) 3 m 85 cm   (d) 3 m 86 cm

US‣ Exercise 8

1. 950 m - 50 m   860 m – 140 m   570 m – 430 m   650 m – 350 m
   480 m – 520 m   820 m – 180 m   210 m – 790 m   670 m – 330 m

2. (a) 20   (b) 110   (c) 210
   (d) 580   (e) 80   (f) 120

3. (a) 608 km   (b) Malacca, 82 km

4. (a) 23 km   (b) 90 km   (c) 65 km   (d) 19 km   (e) 6 km

5. (a) 2000   (b) 4000   (c) 5000   (d) 8000

6. (a) 3   (b) 6   (c) 7   (d) 9

7. (a) 1145   (b) 3050   (c) 1298   (d) 2078
   (e) 2580   (f) 1006   (g) 3670

8. (a) 1 km 732 m   (b) 1 km 305 m
   (c) 2 km 245 m   (d) 1 km 300 m
   (e) 3 km 260 m   (f) 3 km 6 m
   (g) 2 km 108 m

9. (a) longer than   (b) longer than   (c) shorter than

10. (a) 741 m
    (b) 1 km 865 m or 1865 m
    (c) well, 1 km 124 m or 1124 m
    (d) 1 km 936 m or 1936 m
    (e) 2 km 601 m

3d➤ Exercise 8

1. 950 m - 50 m   860 m – 140 m   570 m – 430 m   650 m – 350 m
    480 m – 520 m   820 m – 180 m   210 m – 790 m   670 m – 330 m
2. (a) 20   (b) 110   (c) 210
    (d) 580   (e) 80   (f) 120

3d➤ Exercise 9

1. (a) 608 km   (b) Malacca, 82 km

2. (a) 23 km   (b) 90 km   (c) 65 km   (d) 19 km   (e) 6 km

3. (a) 2000   (b) 4000   (c) 5000   (d) 8000
4. (a) 3   (b) 6   (c) 7   (d) 9

3d➤ Exercise 10

1. (a) 1145   (b) 3050   (c) 1298   (d) 2078
    (e) 2580   (f) 1006   (g) 3670

2. (a) 1 km 732 m   (b) 1 km 305 m   (c) 2 km 245 m   (d) 1 km 300 m
    (e) 3 km 260 m   (f) 3 km 6 m   (g) 2 km 108 m

3. (a) longer than   (b) longer than   (c) shorter than

4. (a) 741 m
    (b) 1 km 865 m or 1865 m
    (c) well, 1 km 124 m or 1124 m
    (d) 1 km 936 m or 1936 m
    (e) 2 km 601 m

US➤ Exercise 9
3d➤ Exercise 11

1. (a) 1 km 850 m   (b) 3 km 180 m   (c) 5 km 230 m

2. (a) 6 km 110 m
   (b) 7 km 970 m   (c) 10 km 200 m (d) 6 km 150 m
   (e) 9 km 200 m   (f) 11 km 100 m

3. (a) 2 km 70 m
   (b) 3 km 940 m   (c) 5 km 260 m

4. (a) 2 km 650 m
   (b) 5 km 920 m   (c) 3 km 750 m   (d) 6 km 920 m

US➤ Exercise 10

1. (a) 29   (b) 10   (c) 381   (d) 602

2. (a) 5 yd 0 ft (b) 8 yd 1 ft (c) 101 yd 2 ft (d) 200 yd 0 ft

3. (a) 23   (b) 101   (c) 122
   (d) 34   (e) 81   (f) 108

4. (a) equal to (1 ft 3 in. = 15 in.)   (b) shorter than (1 yd 2 ft = 5 ft)
   (c) longer than (5 ft 11 in. = 71 in.)   (d) longer than (1 yd 2 ft = 5 ft)
   (e) equal to (5 yd 1 ft = 16 ft)   (f) shorter than (2 ft 2 in. = 26 in.)

5. (a) 450 ft + 361 ft = 811 ft or 270 yd 1 ft
   (b) 678 ft + 107 ft = 785 ft or 261 yd 2 ft
   (c) D; 22 ft or 7 yd 1 ft
        43 yd = 129 ft; 129 ft – 107 ft = 22 ft
        or 107 ft = 35 yd 2 ft; 43 yd – 35 yd 2 ft = 7 yd 1 ft
   (d) 450 ft + 678 ft = 1128 ft

Exercise 10a (in appendix)

1. (a) 32   (b) 19   (c) 36   (d) 452

2. (a) 47   (b) 116   (c) 125   (d) 94

3. (a) 1 ft 5 in. (b) 4 ft 0 in. (c) 2 ft 2 in.

4. (a) 6 yd 2 ft (c) 14 yd 0 ft (c) 68 yd 2 ft (d) 133 yd 1 ft

5. (a) 1 m, 39 in., 4 ft, 1 yd 2 ft
   (b) 10 cm, 1 ft 10 in., 2 ft, 26 in.

6. (a) 342 ft + 320 ft = 662 ft
         662 ft = **220 yd 2 ft**

    (b) 66 yd = 198 ft
         198 ft + 478 ft = **676 ft**

    (c) 10 ft; 3 yd 1 ft

    (d) total distance = 798 ft
         798 ft = **266 yd 0 ft**

US> Exercise 11

1. (a) 2 ft 4 in.   (b) 3 ft 7 in.   (c) 6 ft 7 in.   (d) 4 yd 1 ft

2. (a) 5 yd 1 ft   (b) 9 yd 0 ft   (c) 21 yd 1 ft
    (d) 11 ft 5 in.   (e) 13 ft 0 in.   (f) 10 ft 4 in.

3. (a) 2 ft 2 in.   (b) 4 ft 9 in.   (c) 7 ft 11 in.
    (d) 5 yd 0 ft   (e) 1 yd 2 ft

4. (a) 1 yd 2 ft   (b) 1 yd 0 ft   (c) 1 yd 2 ft
    (d) 0 ft 4 in.   (e) 4 ft 8 in.   (f) 0 ft. 10 in.

5. (a) longer than
    (b) longer than

6. (a) 3806 mi + 5950 mi. = **9756 mi**
    (b) 5950 mi. – 3806 mi. = **2144 mi**

Exercise 11a (in appendix)

1. (a) 3 ft 4 in.   (b) 4 ft 8 in.   (c) 5 ft 3 in.   (d) 6 yd 1 ft
    (e) 11 yd 1 ft   (f) 20 yd 2 ft   (g) 31 yd 1 ft   (h) 10 ft 6 in.
    (i) 12 ft 0 in.   (j) 20 ft 5 in.   (k) 29 ft 3 in.   (l) 375 ft 8 in.

2. (a) 3 ft 2 in.   (b) 5 ft 9 in.   (c) 9 ft 11 in.   (d) 6 yd 0 ft
    (e) 7 yd 2 ft   (f) 2 yd 1 ft   (g) 11 yd 2 ft   (h) 11 yd 2 ft
    (i) 4 ft 4 in.   (j) 7 ft 1 in.   (k) 10 ft 10 in.   (l) 17 ft 4 in.

3. 30 inches = 2 ft 6 in.
    Length to be removed = 6 ft 3 in. – 2 ft 6 in. = **3 ft 9 in.**

4. Total distance = 12 ft 4 in. + 24 ft 8 in. = 36 ft 12 in. = **12 yd 1 ft**

5. (a) Distance from Boston to Seattle = 1390 mi + 1650 mi = **3040 mi**
    (b) Difference in distance = 1650 mi – 1390 mi = **260 mi**

Exercise 12

2. (a) 2 kg 500 g　(b) 1 kg 200 g

3. (a) 1 kg 400 g　(b) 2 kg 700 g　(c) 1 kg 700 g　(d) 3 kg 700 g

---

US▸ Exercise 13

1. (a) 1 kg　(b) 200 g　(c) 550 g　(d) 330 g
   (e) 250 g　(f) 610 g　(g) 850 g　(h) 780 g

2. 9 kg 950 g → 9950 g　9 kg 95 g → 9095 g　9 kg 905 g → 9905 g
   9 kg 59 g → 9059 g　9 kg 590 g → 9590 g

3. 1 kg 10 g → 1010 g　1 kg 100 g → 1100 g　1 kg 250 g → 1250 g
   1 kg 25 g → 1025 g　2 kg 25 g → 2025 g　2 kg 50 g → 2050 g
   3 kg 80 g → 3080 g　3 kg 8 g → 3008 g

4. (a) 1800　(b) 6020　(c) 2300
   (d) 9002　(e) 4083　(f) 8015

5. (a) 1 kg 280 g　(b) 4 kg 69 g　(c) 2 kg 506 g
   (d) 5 kg 108 g　(e) 3 kg 9 g　(f) 6 kg 4 g

6. (a) lighter than　(b) equal to　(c) lighter than　(d) equal to

7. (a) hen, duck　(b) A, B

8. (a) D　(b) B　(c) B　(d) D

3d▸ Exercise 13

1. (a) 1 kg　(b) 200 g　(c) 550 g　(d) 330 g
   (e) 250 g　(f) 610 g　(g) 850 g　(h) 780 g

2. 9 kg 950 g → 9950 g　9 kg 95 g → 9095 g　9 kg 905 g → 9905 g
   9 kg 59 g → 9059 g　9 kg 590 g → 9590 g

3. 1 kg 10 g → 1010 g　1 kg 100 g → 1100 g　1 kg 250 g → 1250 g
   1 kg 25 g → 1025 g　2 kg 25 g → 2025 g　2 kg 50 g → 2050 g
   3 kg 80 g → 3080 g　3 kg 8 g → 3008 g

3d▸ Exercise 14

1. (a) 1800   (b) 6020   (c) 2300
   (d) 9002   (e) 4083   (f) 8015

2. (a) 1 kg 280 g   (b) 4 kg 69 g   (c) 2 kg 506 g
   (d) 5 kg 108 g   (e) 3 kg 9 g   (f) 6 kg 4 g

3. (a) lighter than   (b) equal to   (c) lighter than   (d) equal to

4. (a) hen, duck   (b) A, B

5. (a) D   (b) B   (c) B   (d) D

US▸ Exercise 14
3d▸ Exercise 15

1. (a) 1 kg 850 g   (b) 3 kg 250 g   (c) 4 kg 280 g

2. (a) 3 kg 765 g   (b) 6 kg 250 g   (c) 6 kg 55 g   (d) 8 kg 9 g

3. (a) 4 kg 90 g   (b) 4 kg 545 g   (c) 6 kg 635 g

4. (a) 1 kg 156 g   (b) 2 kg 742 g   (c) 850 g   (d) 6 kg 736 g

---

US▸ Exercise 15
3d▸ Exercise 16

1. (a) 280 g   (b) 280 g – 100 g = 180 g

2. (a) 370 g   (b) 370 g – 150 g = 220 g

3. (a) 330 g   (b) 330 g – 130 g = 200 g
   (c) 200 g ÷ 2 = 100 g

4. (a) 330 g   (b) 60 g x 2 = 120 g, 330 g – 120 g = 210 g
   (c) 210 g ÷ 5 = 42 g

5. (a) 5 kg   (b) $5 ÷ 5 = $1

6. (a) 2 kg   (b) $6 ÷ 2 = $3

US▸ Exercise 16

1. (a) 3 lb 8 oz   (b) 6 lb 10 oz

2. (a) 32 oz   (b) 58 oz   (c) 137 oz

3. (a) 1 lb 2 oz   (b) 1 lb 6 oz   (c) 2 lb 0 oz

4. (a) heavier than   (b) lighter than   (c) equal to   (d) heaver than

5. (a) 13 lb 1 oz   (b) 12 lb 0 oz   (c) 7 lb 1 oz

6. (a) 2 lb 6 oz   (b) 1 lb 14 oz   (c) 0 lb 15 oz

7. (a) 3 lb   (b) Cost of 1 lb = $9 ÷ 3 = **$3**

8. 17 lb 1 oz

Exercise 16a (in appendix)

1. (a) 7 lb 10 oz   (b) 2 lb 8 oz

2. (a) 48 oz   (b) 102 oz
    (c) 138 oz   (d) 82 oz
    (e) 1 lb 2 oz   (f) 2 lb 0 oz

3. 1 gram, 21 oz, 1 lb 7 oz, 1 kilogram

4. (a) 14 lb 1 oz   (b) 20 lb 0 oz   (c) 56 lb 3 oz
    (d) 6 lb 5 oz   (e) 21 lb 14 oz   (f) 1 lb 4 oz

5. Weight of smaller watermelon = 20 lb – 13 lb 9 oz = **6 lb 7 oz**

6. Weight of bananas = 4 oz + 10 oz = 14 oz
    Weight of gapes = 14 lb + 14 lb 14 lb = 1 lb 12 oz + 14 lb = **2 lb 10 oz**

Review 1

1. odd: 9, 13, 127, 1229   even: 6, 72, 354, 1350

2. 800, 400, 300, 60, 10

3. (a) 6250   (b) 45,403   (c) 5000   (d) 2009

3d➤4. (a) 8   (b) 45   (c) 65   (d) 930   (e) 310
       (f) 520   (g) 940   (h) 210   (i) 160
US➤4. (a) 8   (b) 45   (c) 3   (d) 930   (e) 310
       (f) 1   (g) 940   (h) 210   (i) 8

5. Distance = 3 km 120 m – 1 km 250 m = **1 km 870 m**

3d➤6. Total weight = 2 kg 750 g + 2 kg 860 g = **5 kg 610 g**
US➤6. Total weight = 2 lb 8 oz + 2 lb 9 oz = **5 lb 1 oz**

7. Total weight 9 x 256 g = 2304 g = **2 kg 304 g**

8. Cost of 1 kg = $8 ÷ 4 = **$2**

9. Cost of storybooks = $12 x 7 = $84
    Total cost = $84 + $25 = **$109**

10. 4 people paid $12
    1 person paid $12 ÷ 4 = **$8.00**

Review 2

1. Cost of 5 books = $90
   Cost of 1 book = $90 ÷ 5 = **$18**

2. Smaller number = 120 – 50 = **70**

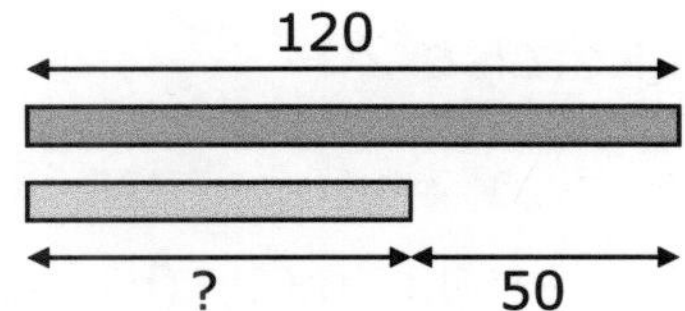

3. 72 ÷ 8 = 9. The length is **9 times** as long.

4. Total distance = 3 km 300 m + 1 km 500 m = **4 km 800 m**

3d➤5. Total flour used = 3 kg 500 g + 800 g = **4 kg 300 g**
US➤5. Total flour used = 6 lb 8 oz + 12 oz = **7 lb 4 oz**

6. Number sold Monday = 402 – 35 = 367
   Total sold = 402 + 367 = **769**

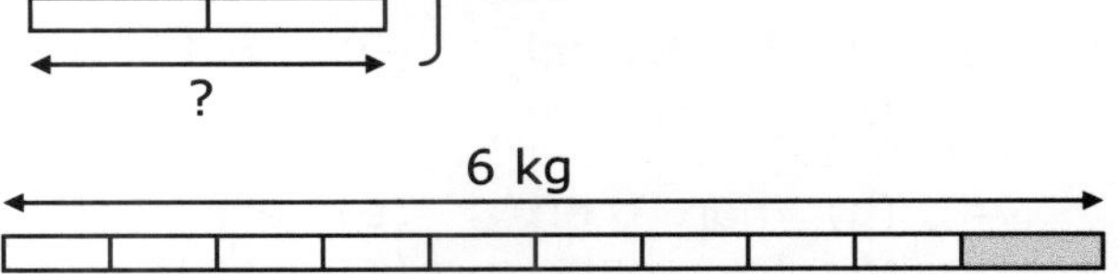

7. 3 units = 180
   1 unit = 180 ÷ 3 = 60
   2 units = 60 x 2 = 120
   The larger number is **120**

8. Weight of 9 fish = 9 x 628 g
                     = 5652 g
                     = 5 kg 652 g
   Weight of prawns = 6 kg – 5 kg 652 g = **348 g**

9. Total meters = 125 m + 215 m = 340 m
   Total cost = 340 x $5 = **$1700**
   Or Cost of red cloth = 125 x $5 = $625
      Cost of blue cloth = 215 x $5 = $1075
      Total cost = $625 + $1075 = $1700

Exercise 17

1. (c) 1000

2. 5

Exercise 19

1. left side: 300 ml, 1ℓ, 400 ml, 800 ml, 700 ml
   right side: 100 ml, 600 ml, 200 ml, 500 ml, 900 ml

2. (a) 400 ml   (b) 700 ml

    (c) 350 ml   (d) 150 ml
    (e) 30 ml   (f) 800 ml

Exercise 20

1. 890 → 110   725 → 275   495 → 505   645 → 355

2. (a) 930 ml   (b) 450 ml   (c) 370 ml   (d) 920 ml

3. (a) 140 ml   (b) 580 ml   (c) 250 ml   (d) 660 ml

Exercise 21

1. 2ℓ = 2000 ml 1ℓ 120 ml = 1120 ml
   1ℓ 35 ml = 1035 ml 1ℓ 350 ml = 1350 ml
   2ℓ 500 ml = 2500 ml 2ℓ 50 ml = 2050 ml

2. (a) 1100   (b) 1725   (c) 1640
   (d) 2855   (e) 2025   (f) 3005

3. (a) 1ℓ 300 ml   (b) 1ℓ 450 ml   (c) 2ℓ 90 ml
   (d) 2ℓ 105 ml   (e) 3ℓ 75 ml   (f) 4ℓ 5 ml

4. (a) more than   (b) less than   (c) equal to
   (d) less than   (e) less than

US⟩ Exercise 22

1. (a) 1ℓ 750 ml
   (b) 3ℓ 0 ml   (c) 4ℓ 150 ml   (d) 5ℓ 490 ml

2. (a) 3ℓ 760 ml
   (b) 3ℓ 890 ml   (c) 5ℓ 70 ml   (d) 6ℓ 45 ml   (e) 8ℓ 14 ml

3. (a) 3ℓ 180 ml
   (b) 4ℓ 40 ml   (c) 4ℓ 670 ml   (d) 5ℓ 950 ml

4. (a) 2ℓ 180 ml
   (b) 1ℓ 64 ml   (c) 2ℓ 665 ml   (d) 760 ml   (e) 5ℓ 721 ml

5. (a) $3\ell - 1\ell$ 50 ml = **1ℓ 950 ml**
   (b) $3\ell + 1\ell$ 50 ml = **4ℓ 50 ml**

6. (a) $5\ell - 3\ell = \mathbf{2\ell}$
   (b) $5\ell + 2\ell + 3\ell = \mathbf{10\ell}$
   (c) $10\ell - 8\ell$ 400 ml = **1ℓ 600 ml**

7. Total milk = 375 ml x 6 = 2250 ml = **2ℓ 250 ml**

8. Total paint = 3ℓ x 4 = 12ℓ
    Paint used = 12ℓ – 2ℓ 450 ml = **9ℓ 550 ml**

3d➤ Exercise 22

1. (a) 1ℓ 750 ml
    (b) 3ℓ 0 ml   (c) 4ℓ 150 ml   (d) 5ℓ 490 ml

2. (a) 3ℓ 760 ml
    (b) 3ℓ 890 ml   (c) 5ℓ 70 ml   (d) 6ℓ 45 ml   (e) 8ℓ 14 ml

3. (a) 3ℓ 180 ml
    (b) 4ℓ 40 ml   (c) 4ℓ 670 ml   (d) 5ℓ 950 ml

4. (a) 2ℓ 180 ml
    (b) 1ℓ 64 ml   (c) 2ℓ 665 ml   (d) 760 ml   (e) 5ℓ 721 ml

---

3d➤ Exercise 23

1. (a) 3ℓ – 1ℓ 50 ml = **1ℓ 950 ml**
    (b) 3ℓ + 1ℓ 50 ml = **4ℓ 50 ml**

2. (a) 5ℓ – 3 ℓ = **2ℓ**
    (b) 5ℓ + 2ℓ + 3ℓ = **10ℓ**
    (c) 10ℓ – 8ℓ 400 ml = **1ℓ 600 ml**

3. Total milk = 375 ml x 6 = 2250 ml = **2ℓ 250 ml**

4. Total paint = 3ℓ x 4 = 12ℓ
    Paint used = 12ℓ – 2ℓ 450 ml = **9ℓ 550 ml**

US➤ Exercise 23

1. 3 pt → 6 c   16 c → 1 gal   2 qt → 4 pt
    1 gal 3 qt → 7 qt   4 pt 1 c → 9 c   5 qt 1 pt → 11 pt

2. (a) 9 pt 0 c   (b) 15 gal 2 qt

3. (a) 1 gal 2 qt   (b) 6 qt 1 pt

4. (a) equal to   (b) more than   (c) less than   (d) more than

5. (a) 15 gal 2 qt – 6 gal 3 qt = **8 gal 3 qt**
    (b) 15 gal 2 qt + 6 gal 3 qt = **22 gal 1 qt**

Exercise 23a (in appendix)

1. (a) <   (b) <   (c) >   (d) =
2. 1 liter, 4 pt 1 c, 1 gal 2 c, 20 c,
3. (a) 19 pt 0 c   (b) 22 gal 2 qt
    (c) 1 gal 2 qt (d) 20 qt 1 c
4. (a) Total capacity = 15 gal 2 qt + 14 gal 3 qt = **30 gal 1 qt**
    (b) Difference = 15 gal 2 qt − 14 gal 3 qt = **3 qt**

Exercise 24

1. (a) 10   (b) 6:45 a.m. (c) 4   (d) 6:30 a.m. (e) 18
2. (a) 4   (b) 2   (c) 62
3. (a) 650   (b) 150   (c) Wed.   (d) Mon.   (e) 2200

Exercise 25

1. (a) 12   (b) Mary, 18 (c) Weilin, 9 (d) 2   (e) Weilin
3d▸2. (a) $45   (b) $10   (c) Raju   (d) Raju   (e) $185
US▸2. (a) $45   (b) $10   (c) Ryan   (d) Ryan   (e) $185

3. (a) 180   (b) 120   (c) Samy   (d) John   (e) 160

Review 3

1. 66 → 34   53 → 47   38 → 62   55 → 45   18 → 82   26 → 74
2. $7.80 → $2.20 $8.75 → $1.25 $6.55 → $3.45
    $5.65 → $4.35 $4.95 → $5.05 $9.30 → $0.70
3. (a) 310   (b) 2 m 85 cm
    (c) 4050 g   (d) 3 kg 50 g
    (e) 2005 m   (f) 2 km 500 m
    (g) 3060 ml   (h) 4ℓ 5 ml
4. (a) 7 m 45 cm   (b) 3 km 985 m
    (c) 5 kg 170 g   (d) 2ℓ 960 ml
5. (a) 1ℓ 400 ml   (b) 1ℓ   (c) 200 ml
6. (a) 50   (b) 300
7. Number of females = 6523 − 3806 = **2717**

8. Number of pies packed into boxes = 157 − 37 = 120
   Number of boxes = 120 ÷ 8 = **15**

9. Cost of photo album = $12.50 + $3.50 = $16.00
   Total cost = $16.00 + $12.50 = **$28.50**

Review 4

1. (a) 3010   (b) 6000   (c) 4015
   (d) 2308   (e) 1968   (f) 2354

2. (a) 406   (b) 848   (c) 2304
   (d) 28   (e) 38   (f) 50 r2

3. (a) Amount cheaper = $10.40 − $8.60 = **$1.90**
   (b) Total spent = $36.90 + $40.80 + $38.40 = **$106.10**
   (c) Cost = $8.95 + $8.60 + $10.50 = $28.05
   3d➤ Change = $50 − $28.05 = **$21.95**
   US➤ Change = $40 - $28.05 = **$11.95**

3d➤4. Amount left = 1 ℓ − 250 ml = **750 ml**
US➤4. Amount left = 1 qt − 1 c = **3 c**

5. Total = 4328 + 5860 = **10,188**

6. Number each child got = 204 ÷ 3 = **68**

7. Cost of both = $1.25 + $12.50 = $13.75
   Change = $20 − $13.75 = **$6.25**

8. 1 unit = cost of calculator
   1 unit = $164 ÷ 4 = $41
   Total cost = 5 units
   5 units = $41 x 5 = $205
   Or: Total cost = $164 + $41 = **$205**

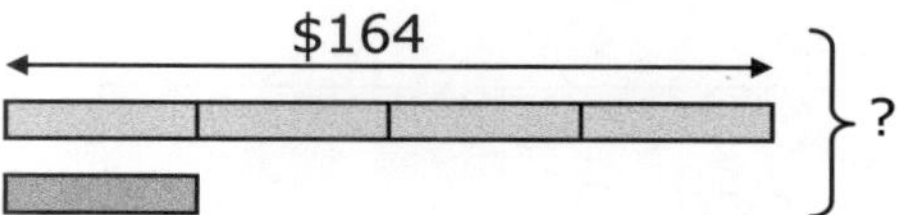

Exercise 26

1. $\dfrac{1}{3}$, $\dfrac{2}{5}$, $\dfrac{3}{8}$, $\dfrac{3}{4}$, $\dfrac{4}{5}$, $\dfrac{5}{8}$

2. (a) $\dfrac{2}{3}$ (b) $\dfrac{7}{8}$ (c) $\dfrac{5}{9}$ (d) $\dfrac{7}{10}$

Exercise 27

1. (a) 3, 4   (b) 4, 3   (c) $\frac{1}{4}$

2. (a) 4, 6   (b) 6, 4   (c) $\frac{2}{6}$

3. (a) 3, 10   (b) 10, 3   (c) $\frac{7}{10}$

4. (a) $\frac{1}{5}$ (b) $\frac{4}{9}$

5. $\frac{4}{7} \to \frac{3}{7}$ $\frac{5}{7} \to \frac{2}{7}$ $\frac{7}{8} \to \frac{1}{8}$

   $\frac{3}{8} \to \frac{5}{8}$ $\frac{9}{10} \to \frac{1}{10}$ $\frac{7}{10} \to \frac{3}{10}$

Exercise 28

1. (a) $\frac{2}{3}$ (b) $\frac{3}{4}$ (c) $\frac{3}{5}$

   (d) $\frac{4}{6}$ (e) $\frac{5}{8}$ (f) $\frac{5}{9}$

2. (a) 4, 4, 2   (b) 5, 5, 4   (c) 6, 6, 3
   (d) 8, 8, 7   (e) 10, 10, 6   (f) 12, 12, 9

Exercise 29

1. (a) $\frac{1}{3}$ (b) $\frac{1}{6}$ (c) $\frac{3}{4}$ (d) $\frac{2}{3}$

2. (a) $\frac{1}{6}$ (b) $\frac{1}{5}$ (c) $\frac{5}{8}$ (d) $\frac{3}{10}$

3. (a) $\frac{1}{7}$ (b) $\frac{1}{8}$ (c) $\frac{6}{7}$ (d) $\frac{7}{8}$

4. (a) $\frac{1}{5}$ (b) $\frac{1}{10}$ (c) $\frac{3}{7}$ (d) $\frac{5}{12}$

5. (a) $\frac{1}{10}, \frac{1}{7}, \frac{1}{6}$ (b) $\frac{3}{10}, \frac{3}{8}, \frac{3}{4}$ (c) $\frac{1}{9}, \frac{1}{5}, 1$

6. (a) $\frac{1}{3}, \frac{1}{4}, \frac{1}{12}$ (b) $\frac{5}{7}, \frac{5}{9}, \frac{5}{12}$ (c) $\frac{1}{8}, \frac{1}{10}, 0$

Exercise 30

1. (a) $\dfrac{4}{6}$, $\dfrac{5}{6}$ (b) $\dfrac{5}{8}$, $\dfrac{6}{8}$ (c) $\dfrac{8}{12}$, $\dfrac{10}{12}$, 1

   (d) $\dfrac{6}{9}$, $\dfrac{5}{9}$, $\dfrac{4}{9}$ (e) $\dfrac{6}{10}$, $\dfrac{5}{10}$, $\dfrac{4}{10}$

2. (a) $\dfrac{5}{8}$ (b) $\dfrac{2}{6}$ (c) $\dfrac{4}{5}$ (d) $\dfrac{7}{10}$

3. (a) $\dfrac{4}{5}$ (b) $\dfrac{6}{7}$ (c) $\dfrac{7}{10}$ (d) $\dfrac{5}{6}$

4. (a) $\dfrac{1}{3}$ (b) $\dfrac{1}{5}$ (c) $\dfrac{4}{10}$ (d) $\dfrac{5}{12}$

5. (a) $\dfrac{4}{5}$ (b) $\dfrac{6}{7}$ (c) $\dfrac{8}{9}$ (d) $\dfrac{10}{12}$

6. (a) $\dfrac{1}{4}$ (b) $\dfrac{2}{6}$ (c) $\dfrac{4}{10}$ (d) $\dfrac{2}{11}$

7. (a) $\dfrac{3}{10}$, $\dfrac{5}{10}$, $\dfrac{8}{10}$ (b) $\dfrac{3}{12}$, $\dfrac{5}{12}$, 1

Exercise 31

1. $\dfrac{5}{6} \to \dfrac{10}{12}$ $\dfrac{2}{3} \to \dfrac{6}{9}$ $\dfrac{5}{10} \to \dfrac{1}{2}$ $\dfrac{3}{5} \to \dfrac{6}{10}$

2. (a) 2   (b) 3   (c) 5
   (d) 2   (e) 4   (f) 10
   (g) 2   (h) 3   (i) 6
   (j) 2   (k) 4   (l) 8

Exercise 32

1. (a) 6; 3   (b) 6; 12   (c) 3; 6

2. (a) $\dfrac{8}{10}$ (b) $\dfrac{4}{12}$

3. $\dfrac{1}{2}$, $\dfrac{2}{4}$ $\dfrac{4}{5}$, $\dfrac{8}{10}$ $\dfrac{1}{4}$, $\dfrac{2}{8}$ $\dfrac{6}{10}$, $\dfrac{3}{5}$

   $\dfrac{2}{6}$, $\dfrac{1}{3}$ $\dfrac{1}{2}$, $\dfrac{5}{10}$ $\dfrac{2}{6}$, $\dfrac{3}{9}$

Exercise 33

1. (a) $\frac{4}{5}$ (b) $\frac{5}{6}$

   (c) $\frac{3}{4}$ (d) $\frac{8}{10}$

   (e) $\frac{1}{2}$ (f) $\frac{2}{3}$

   (g) $\frac{6}{12}$ (h) $\frac{2}{3}$

2. (a) $\frac{4}{6}$ (b) $\frac{8}{10}$ (c) $\frac{2}{5}$ (d) $\frac{6}{6}$

   (e) $\frac{3}{4}$ (f) $\frac{2}{12}$ (g) $\frac{3}{4}$ (h) $\frac{5}{10}$

Exercise 34

1. (a) $\frac{2}{3}$ (b) $\frac{3}{4}$

2. (a) $\frac{1}{2}$ (b) $\frac{2}{3}$ (c) $\frac{1}{3}$

3. Lucky

4. (1) $\frac{2}{3}$ (2) $\frac{1}{3}$ (3) $\frac{1}{5}$ (4) $\frac{1}{4}$ (5) $\frac{1}{2}$

   (6) $\frac{4}{5}$ (7) $\frac{3}{4}$ (8) $\frac{5}{6}$ (9) $\frac{1}{6}$ WATER POLO

Exercise 35

1. (a) $\frac{7}{8}$ (b) $\frac{4}{5}$

   (c) $\frac{2}{3}$ (d) $\frac{2}{3}$

   (e) $\frac{4}{5}$ (f) $\frac{11}{12}$

   (g) $\frac{2}{3}$ (h) $\frac{1}{2}$

2. (a) $\dfrac{2}{5}$, $\dfrac{1}{2}$, $\dfrac{5}{6}$ (b) $\dfrac{1}{2}$, $\dfrac{5}{8}$, $\dfrac{3}{4}$

(c) $\dfrac{7}{12}$, $\dfrac{2}{3}$, $\dfrac{5}{6}$ (d) $\dfrac{7}{12}$, $\dfrac{2}{3}$, $\dfrac{3}{4}$

Review 5

1. (a) 60   (b) 300   (c) 70   (d) 500

2. (a) x   (b) –   (c) ÷   (d) +   (e) –

3. Total amount she earned = 9 x \$45 = **\$405**

4. Difference in weight = 2 x 29 kg = **58 kg**

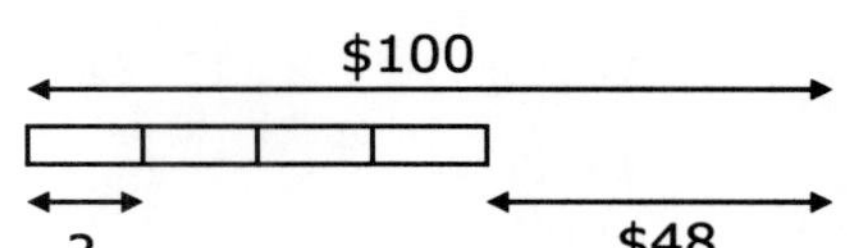

5. Total tiles used = 1164 + 940 = 2104
Tiles left = 2500 – 2104 = **396**

6. Total women = 2000 – 1340 = 660
Number more men than women = 1340 – 660 = **680**

7. Jim jogged a longer distance
3 km 600 m – 2 km 800 m = **800 m**

8. Cost of present = \$100 - \$48 = \$52
Amount each person paid = \$52 ÷ 4 = **\$13**

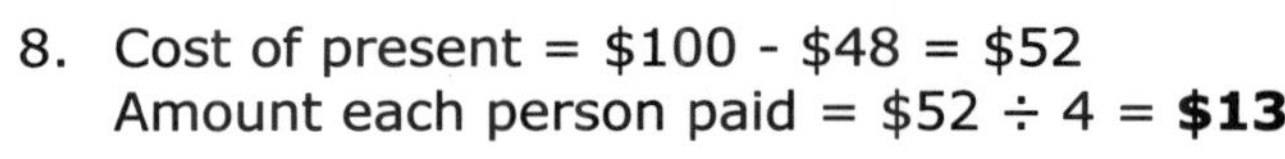

9. Total = 8 x 12 = 96
Number eaten = 96 – 28 = **68**

10. Weight of sand = 5 kg – 200 g = **4 kg 800 g**

3d➤11. Brother's height = 1 m 57 cm – 25 cm = **1 m 32 cm**
US➤11. Brother's height = 4 ft 1 in – 5 in = **3 ft 8 in.**

12. 3 units = 240
2 unit = 240 ÷ 3 = 80
One number = 1 unit = **80**
Other number = 2 units = 2 x 80 = **160**

Review 6

1. (a) 185   (b) 53   (c) 6700
(d) 2972   (e) 3654   (f) 2304

3. (a) $\dfrac{1}{4}$ (b) $\dfrac{3}{8}$ (c) $\dfrac{2}{3}$

(d) $\dfrac{4}{6}$ (e) $\dfrac{3}{4}$ (f) $\dfrac{3}{8}$

5. Amount = $85 x 3 = **$255**

3d▸6. Cards Gopal collected = 4 units = 48
    Cards Raju collected = 1 unit = 48 ÷ 4 = **12**
US▸6. Cards Gary collected = 4 units = 48
    Cards Ryan collected = 1 unit = 48 ÷ 4 = **12**

3d▸7. Amount of flour she had left = 1 kg – 450 g = **550 g**
US▸7. Amount of flour she had left = 1 lb – 9 oz = **7 oz**

8. Weight of 8 packets of onions
    = 8 x 450 g
    = 3600 g
    = 3 kg 600 g
    Weight of potatoes = 5 kg – 3 kg 600 g = **1 kg 400 g**

9. (a) Cost of 4 rolls = 5 x $4 = **$20**
    (b) Cost for 1 bow = $20 ÷ 10 = **$2**

Exercise 36

1. 7:17   8:03
    2:41   4:36
    4:02   8:14
    11:52   12:21

2. 12:00
    noon

    4:42   9:10   2:45
    18 minutes to 5   10 minutes past 9   15 minutes to 3

    4:55   11:05   1:27
    5 minutes to 5   5 minutes past 11   27 minutes past 1

    7:25   10:36   8:53
    25 minutes past 7   24 minutes to 11   7 minutes to 9

Exercise 37

1. (a) 25   (b) 30, 6:05
    (c) 6:10, 2, 8:10   (d) 7:25, 3, 10:25

2. (a) 1 h 15 min   (b) 2:20, 3 h 50, 6:10
    (c) 7:40, 8 h , 3:40   (d) 8:50, 4 h 25 min, 1:15

Exercise 38

1.
                                                   90 min → 1 h 30 min

    120 min → 2 h   110 min → 1 h 50 min

    130 min → 2 h 10 min   95 min → 1 h 35 min

    135 min → 2 h 15 min   210 min → 3 h 30 min

2. (a) 105   (b) 125

     (c) 1 h 25 min   (d) 2 h 30 min

3. (a) 65   (b) 90

     (c) 145   (d) 190

4. (a) 1 h 15 min   (b) 1 h 40 min

     (c) 2 h 20 min   (d) 3 h 45 min

Exercise 39

1. 9:15 p.m.

2. 1 h 20 min

3. 7:10 p.m.

4. 1 h 20 min

5. 8:20 a.m.

6. 25 min

Exercise 40

1. (a) 1 h 55 min   (b) 2 h 25 min

     (c) 3 h 20 min   (d) 3 h 10 min

2. (a) 4 h 10 min   (b) 3 h 10 min

     (c) 4 h 10 min   (d) 4 h 15 min

     (e) 5 h 10 min   (f) 6 h 10 min

3. (a) 1 h 35 min   (b) 2 h 25 min

     (c) 1 h 15 min   (d) 2 h 55 min

4. (a) 1 h 20 min   (b) 1 h 5 min

     (c) 1 h 15 min   (d) 1 h 30 min

     (e) 1 h 45 min   (f) 2 h 55 min

Exercise 41

3d> 2. (a) Devi (b) Sulin (c) 4
US> 2. (a) Emily (b) Taylor (c) 4

3. (a) 20 (b) 26 (c) 45 (d) 34

Exercise 42

1. 60 s, 65 s, 105 s, 120 s, 145 s, 180 s, 215 s

2. (a) 100 s (b) 130 s
 (c) 1 min 40 s (d) 2 min 30 s

3. (a) 85 s (b) 165 s (c) 170 s (d) 210 s

4. (a) 1 min 30 s (b) 1 min 55 s (c) 2 min 5 s (d) 3 min 20 s

5. (a) 90 s (b) 115 s
 (c) 125 s (d) 150 s
 (e) 185 s (f) 220 s
 (g) 1 min 20 s (h) 1 min 25 s
 (i) 1 min 35 s (j) 1 m 50 s
 (k) 2 m 20 s (l) 2 m 45 s

Exercise 43

1. 13, 18, 24, 20, 30, 36, 26

2. (a) 17 months (b) 2 years 4 months

3. (a) 15 months (b) 29 months
 (c) 35 months (d) 46 months

4. (a) 1 year 3 months (b) 2 years 1 month
 (c) 2 years 8 months (d) 3 years 4 months

Exercise 44

1. 7, 10, 14, 13, 16, 20, 22

2. (a) 17 days (b) 5 weeks 5 days

3. (a) 12 days (b) 18 days
 (c) 24 days (d) 30 days

4. (a) 1 week 5 days (b) 3 weeks 4 days
 (c) 4 weeks 2 days (d) 4 weeks 4 days

Review 7

1. (a) $\frac{7}{10}$ (b) $\frac{5}{6}$
   (c) $\frac{3}{4}$ (d) $\frac{1}{2}$

2. (a) 10:25 a.m.
   (b) 30

3. (a) 4 (b) 30
   (c) 10 (d) 10

4. (a) m (b) ml (c) g (d) ℓ (e) km

5. (a) Total number of children = 10 x 28 = **280**
   (b) Number of boys = total children – number of girls = 280 – 136 = **144**

6. Total money spent = $1.60 + $5.40 = $7.00
   Money left = $20 - $7 = **$13**

Exercise 45

1. A. 4,4 B. 5,5 C. 3,3 D. 4,4 E. 6,6 F. 5,5

Exercise 46

1. (a) smaller (b) equal (c) bigger (d) bigger (e) equal

3. A. 4,4,2 B. 4,4,2 C. 4,4,4
   D. 4,4,2 E. 4,4,2 F. 5,5,3
   G. 3,3,1 H. 4,4,4 I. 4,4,2

Exercise 47

1. A. 9 B. 10 C. 9 D. 12 E. 11 F. 7
2. A. 9 B. 8 C. 9 D. 6 E. 9 F. 10

Exercise 48

1. A. 11 B. 11 C. 10 D. 13 A & B, D, C
2. A. 9 cm^2 B. 5 cm^2 C. 7 cm^2 D. 8 cm^2

Exercise 49

1. (a) 8 cm^2 (b) 12 cm^2 (c) 5 cm^2
   (d) 6 cm^2 (e) 9 cm^2 (f) 8 cm^2

Exercise 50

1. (a) 14 cm   (b) 16 cm   (c) 12 cm
   (d) 14 cm   (e) 9 cm   (f) 11 cm

2. (a)

A	B	C	D	E	F
10 cm^2	13 cm^2	10 cm^2	9 cm^2	8 cm^2	13 cm^2
14 cm	16 cm	16 cm	12 cm	18 cm	16 cm

   (b) A & C   (c) B & C or C & F   (d) B & F

3. (a) 28 cm   (b) 36 cm   (c) 34 m   (d) 37 m

Exercise 51

1. A. 4, 2, 8 cm^2 B. 6, 2, 12 cm^2 C. 7, 3, 21 cm^2
   D. 5, 3, 15 cm^2 E. 4, 3, 12 cm^2

2. A. 5, 2, 10 cm^2 B. 4, 3, 12 cm^2 C. 6, 4, 24 cm^2
   D. 3, 7, 21 cm^2 E. 8, 1, 8 cm^2

Exercise 52

1. (a) 12 cm^2 (b) 24 cm^2 (c) 35 m^2 (d) 54 cm^2
   (e) 40 m^2 (f) 120 cm^2

2. (a) A. 14 m^2, 18 cm   B. 16 m^2, 16 m   C. 16 cm^2, 20 m
       D. 20 m^2, 18 m   E. 12 m^2, 14 m
   (b) E   (c) C   (d) B & C   (e) A & D

Review 8

1. (a) 32, 40, 48   (b) 63, 54, 45
   (c) 175, 195, 215   (d) 1934, 1734, 1534

2. (a) 45   (b) 20   (c) 240

3. (a) 3 h 50 min   (b) 11:35 a.m.

4. (a) 11 cm^2, 16 cm   (b) 7 m^2, 14 m

5. (a) 35 cm   (b) 36 m

Review 9

1. (a) 5000   (b) 50
2. (a) 6   (b) 5   (c) 5
3. (a) $\dfrac{4}{5}$ (b) $\dfrac{3}{4}$ (c) $\dfrac{1}{2}$
4. (a) $\dfrac{2}{6}, \dfrac{3}{6}, \dfrac{5}{6}$ (b) $\dfrac{4}{9}, \dfrac{2}{3}, \dfrac{7}{9}$ (c) $\dfrac{3}{8}, \dfrac{1}{2}, \dfrac{3}{4}$
5. (a) 30 (5 x 6)   (b) 10 (40 ÷ 4)
6. (a) 3 m x 5 m = **15 m²**
   (b) perimeter of rectangle = 16 cm = perimeter of square
       side of square = 16 cm ÷ 4 = 4 cm
       area of square = 4 cm x 4 cm = **16 m²**
7. 1500 ml = **1** ℓ **500** ml
8. b
9. 2 km 750 m – 1 km 900 m = **850 m**
10. Cost of pen = 45¢ x 8 = 360¢ = **$3.60**
11. 6:50 a.m.
12. Total in one box = 8 + 6 = 14
    Total in five boxes = 14 x 5 = **70**
US➤13. (a) 3 lb 3 oz   (b) 16 pt 1 c   (c)   4 ft 6 in.
US➤14. 3 quarters = 75¢
     Total spent = $3.60 + $0.75 = $4.35
     Total left = $6.00 - $4.35 = **$1.65**
US➤15. 5 dimes = 50¢   8 nickels = 40¢
     Total money = $9.85 + $0.50 + $0.40 = **$10.75**
US➤16. Total pints bought = 4 pt
     Pints left = 4 pt – 2 pt = **2 pt**

Mental Math 1

1.	17	16.	378
2.	26	17.	299
3.	92	18.	878
4.	51	19.	289
5.	40	20.	668
6.	47	21.	988
7.	83	22.	37
8.	95	23.	63
9.	89	24.	78
10.	75	25.	143
11.	459	26.	861
12.	255	27.	496
13.	467	28.	110
14.	290	29.	140
15.	970	30.	121

Mental Math 2

1.	141	16.	130
2.	168	17.	127
3.	113	18.	121
4.	139	19.	111
5.	122	20.	113
6.	100	21.	141
7.	100	22.	72
8.	92	23.	187
9.	122	24.	139
10.	108	25.	153
11.	125	26.	113
12.	82	27.	89
13.	110	28.	152
14.	110	29.	143
15.	140	30.	159

Mental Math 3

1.	44	16.	53
2.	93	17.	34
3.	34	18.	78
4.	26	19.	25
5.	19	20.	19
6.	72	21.	47
7.	67	22.	65
8.	46	23.	46
9.	35	24.	68
10.	40	25.	45
11.	43	26.	52
12.	52	27.	34
13.	63	28.	738
14.	33	29.	559
15.	36	30.	127

Mental Math 4

1.	69	16.	15
2.	39	17.	28
3.	34	18.	67
4.	42	19.	59
5.	16	20.	37
6.	57	21.	86
7.	18	22.	8
8.	14	23.	15
9.	4	24.	17
10.	26	25.	13
11.	16	26.	48
12.	53	27.	36
13.	7	28.	58
14.	29	29.	25
15.	16	30.	103

Mental Math 5

1.	425	16.	593
2.	752	17.	771
3.	599	18.	349
4.	83	19.	461
5.	397	20.	818
6.	323	21.	377
7.	458	22.	241
8.	601	23.	227
9.	913	24.	751
10.	484	25.	548
11.	436	26.	586
12.	299	27.	779
13.	551	28.	544
14.	117	29.	535
15.	464	30.	240

Mental Math 6

1.	597	16.	494
2.	607	17.	194
3.	617	18.	810
4.	521	19.	430
5.	914	20.	455
6.	904	21.	6819
7.	867	22.	6832
8.	576	23.	7089
9.	351	24.	7259
10.	421	25.	7380
11.	349	26.	2280
12.	338	27.	2374
13.	558	28.	2920
14.	484	29.	880
15.	345	30.	1664

Mental Math 7			
1.	50	16.	168
2.	45	17.	1700
3.	64	18.	1660
4.	58	19.	3880
5.	26	20.	5610
6.	93	21.	508
7.	163	22.	2508
8.	218	23.	7508
9.	864	24.	1059
10.	1163	25.	799
11.	800	26.	698
12.	680	27.	99
13.	544	28.	5591
14.	346	29.	6966
15.	605	30.	3371

Mental Math 8			
1.	250	16.	6400
2.	540	17.	300
3.	3500	18.	2400
4.	5600	19.	72
5.	480	20.	490
6.	810	21.	400
7.	3600	22.	4200
8.	1800	23.	630
9.	320	24.	2400
10.	4500	25.	1800
11.	2100	26.	280
12.	90	27.	360
13.	2700	28.	1600
14.	1000	29.	800
15.	120	30.	160

Mental Math 9			
1.	80	16.	800
2.	20	17.	70
3.	700	18.	30
4.	700	19.	400
5.	60	20.	90
6.	900	21.	40
7.	600	22.	600
8.	40	23.	600
9.	50	24.	50
10.	600	25.	500
11.	70	26.	90
12.	300	27.	500
13.	6	28.	30
14.	50	29.	300
15.	200	30.	40

Mental Math 10			
1.	240	16.	242
2.	120	17.	1660
3.	79	18.	354
4.	535	19.	123
5.	116	20.	3000
6.	66	21.	490
7.	60	22.	126
8.	43	23.	707
9.	60	24.	500
10.	68	25.	8091
11.	670	26.	50
12.	8000	27.	8010
13.	3938	28.	87
14.	25	29.	38
15.	1102	30.	900

Mental Math 11			
1.	60	13.	186
2.	24	14.	81
3.	108	15.	36
4.	48	16.	249
5.	72	17.	237
6.	36	18.	132
7.	84	19.	189
8.	96	20.	144
9.	120	21.	174
10.	108	22.	228
11.	132	23.	177
12.	144	24.	219
		25.	303

Mental Math 12			
1.	80	15.	276
2.	32	16.	144
3.	48	17.	50
4.	64	18.	75
5.	16	19.	100
6.	112	20.	540
7.	48	21.	552
8.	128	22.	335
9.	112	23.	336
10.	144	24.	180
11.	108	25.	231
12.	48	26.	261
13.	96	27.	186
14.	84	28.	384
		29.	144

Mental Math 13			
1.	8	16.	3000
2.	36	17.	27
3.	4	18.	20
4.	5000	19.	600
5.	6000	20.	16
6.	8	21.	3000
7.	32	22.	24
8.	36	23.	4000
9.	24	24.	160
10.	8	25.	40
11.	4000	26.	18
12.	100	27.	8000
13.	8000	28.	700
14.	6000	29.	32
15.	700	30.	84

Mental Math 14			
1.	30	16.	18:00
2.	45	17.	22:00
3.	15	18.	14:30
4.	25	19.	17:15
5.	10	20.	23:20
6.	35	21.	13:12
7.	50	22.	16:05
8.	20	23.	4:00
9.	40	24.	6:00
10.	18	25.	1:30
11.	52	26.	7:45
12.	33	27.	2:08
13.	2	28.	9:43
14.	44		
15.	27		

Mental Math 15			
1.	480	16.	7
2.	60	17.	2
3.	420	18.	300
4.	3	19.	63
5.	20	20.	49
6.	120	21.	5
7.	360	22.	6
8.	7	23.	48
9.	8	24.	3
10.	24	25.	240
11.	28	26.	6
12.	180	27.	36
13.	540	28.	8
14.	4	29.	35
15.	5	30.	108

Mental Math 1

1. $14 + 3 = $ __________

2. $17 + 9 = $ __________

3. $89 + 3 = $ __________

4. $46 + 5 = $ __________

5. $32 + 8 = $ __________

6. $45 + 2 = $ __________

7. $23 + 60 = $ __________

8. $45 + 50 = $ __________

9. $28 + 61 = $ __________

10. $32 + 43 = $ __________

11. $456 + 3 = $ __________

12. $249 + 6 = $ __________

13. $458 + 9 = $ __________

14. $230 + 60 = $ __________

15. $920 + 50 = $ __________

16. $348 + 30 = $ __________

17. $259 + 40 = $ __________

18. $832 + 46 = $ __________

19. $258 + 31 = $ __________

20. $453 + 215 = $ __________

21. $272 + 716 = $ __________

22. $5 + 32 = $ __________

23. $6 + 57 = $ __________

24. $40 + 38 = $ __________

25. $8 + 135 = $ __________

26. $4 + 857 = $ __________

27. $45 + 451 = $ __________

28. $80 + 30 = $ __________

29. $70 + 70 = $ __________

30. $91 + 30 = $ __________

Mental Math 2

1. $51 + 90 =$ _________
2. $88 + 80 =$ _________
3. $93 + 20 =$ _________
4. $79 + 60 =$ _________
5. $82 + 40 =$ _________
6. $43 + 57 =$ _________
7. $86 + 14 =$ _________
8. $66 + 26 =$ _________
9. $80 + 42 =$ _________
10. $95 + 13 =$ _________
11. $52 + 73 =$ _________
12. $48 + 34 =$ _________
13. $32 + 78 =$ _________
14. $67 + 43 =$ _________
15. $91 + 49 =$ _________
16. $95 + 35 =$ _________
17. $29 + 98 =$ _________
18. $59 + 62 =$ _________
19. $24 + 87 =$ _________
20. $36 + 77 =$ _________
21. $42 + 99 =$ _________
22. $28 + 44 =$ _________
23. $92 + 95 =$ _________
24. $42 + 97 =$ _________
25. $82 + 71 =$ _________
26. $48 + 65 =$ _________
27. $34 + 55 =$ _________
28. $68 + 84 =$ _________
29. $99 + 44 =$ _________
30. $77 + 82 =$ _________

Mental Math 3

1.	49 − 5 = _______	16.	62 − 9 = _______
2.	96 − 3 = _______	17.	43 − 9 = _______
3.	42 − 8 = _______	18.	84 − 6 = _______
4.	33 − 7 = _______	19.	32 − 7 = _______
5.	25 − 6 = _______	20.	23 − 4 = _______
6.	81 − 9 = _______	21.	54 − 7 = _______
7.	73 − 6 = _______	22.	72 − 7 = _______
8.	54 − 8 = _______	23.	55 − 9 = _______
9.	37 − 2 = _______	24.	77 − 9 = _______
10.	60 − 20 = _______	25.	53 − 8 = _______
11.	63 − 20 = _______	26.	94 − 42 = _______
12.	82 − 30 = _______	27.	59 − 25 = _______
13.	94 − 31 = _______	28.	743 − 5 = _______
14.	85 − 52 = _______	29.	566 − 7 = _______
15.	79 − 43 = _______	30.	136 − 9 = _______

Mental Math 4

1. 98 – 29 = ________	16. 83 – 68 = ________
2. 84 – 45 = ________	17. 36 – 8 = ________
3. 73 – 39 = ________	18. 74 – 7 = ________
4. 50 – 8 = ________	19. 87 – 28 = ________
5. 23 – 7 = ________	20. 43 – 6 = ________
6. 66 – 9 = ________	21. 90 – 4 = ________
7. 53 – 35 = ________	22. 27 – 19 = ________
8. 60 – 46 = ________	23. 72 – 57 = ________
9. 42 – 38 = ________	24. 95 – 78 = ________
10. 55 – 29 = ________	25. 48 – 35 = ________
11. 60 – 44 = ________	26. 145 – 97 = ________
12. 92 – 39 = ________	27. 134 – 98 = ________
13. 22 – 15 = ________	28. 157 – 99 = ________
14. 85 – 56 = ________	29. 120 – 95 = ________
15. 32 – 16 = ________	30. 199 – 96 = ________

Mental Math 5

1. 345 + 80 = ________
2. 692 + 60 = ________
3. 639 – 40 = ________
4. 153 – 70 = ________
5. 458 – 61 = ________
6. 231 + 92 = ________
7. 387 + 71 = ________
8. 630 – 29 = ________
9. 951 – 38 = ________
10. 456 + 28 = ________
11. 364 + 72 = ________
12. 259 + 40 = ________
13. 632 – 81 = ________
14. 193 – 76 = ________
15. 506 – 42 = ________
16. 478 + 115 = ________
17. 542 + 229 = ________
18. 963 – 614 = ________
19. 602 – 141 = ________
20. 455 + 363 = ________
21. 159 + 218 = ________
22. 432 – 191 = ________
23. 132 + 95 = ________
24. 850 – 99 = ________
25. 644 – 96 = ________
26. 489 + 97 = ________
27. 283 + 496 = ________
28. 345 + 199 = ________
29. 832 – 297 = ________
30. 439 – 199 = ________

Mental Math 6

1. 569 + 28 = __________

2. 569 + 38 = __________

3. 569 + 48 = __________

4. 457 + 64 = __________

5. 952 − 38 = __________

6. 952 − 48 = __________

7. 952 − 85 = __________

8. 653 − 77 = __________

9. 413 − 62 = __________

10. 358 + 63 = __________

11. 284 + 65 = __________

12. 402 − 64 = __________

13. 640 − 82 = __________

14. 459 + 25 = __________

15. 284 + 61 = __________

16. 532 − 38 = __________

17. 270 − 76 = __________

18. 777 + 33 = __________

19. 381 + 49 = __________

20. 530 − 75 = __________

21. 6789 + 30 = __________

22. 6789 + 43 = __________

23. 6789 + 300 = __________

24. 6789 + 470 = __________

25. 6789 + 591 = __________

26. 2340 − 60 = __________

27. 2440 − 66 = __________

28. 3320 − 400 = __________

29. 1340 − 460 = __________

30. 2130 − 466 = __________

Mental Math 7

1. $100 - 50 =$ _________
2. $100 - 55 =$ _________
3. $100 - 36 =$ _________
4. $100 - 42 =$ _________
5. $100 - 74 =$ _________
6. $100 - 7 =$ _________
7. $200 - 37 =$ _________
8. $300 - 82 =$ _________
9. $900 - 36 =$ _________
10. $1200 - 37 =$ _________
11. $1000 - 200 =$ _________
12. $1000 - 320 =$ _________
13. $1000 - 456 =$ _________
14. $1000 - 654 =$ _________
15. $1000 - 395 =$ _________
16. $1000 - 832 =$ _________
17. $2000 - 300 =$ _________
18. $2000 - 340 =$ _________
19. $4000 - 120 =$ _________
20. $6000 - 390 =$ _________
21. $1000 - 492 =$ _________
22. $3000 - 492 =$ _________
23. $8000 - 492 =$ _________
24. $2000 - 941 =$ _________
25. $1000 - 201 =$ _________
26. $1000 - 302 =$ _________
27. $800 - 701 =$ _________
28. $6000 - 409 =$ _________
29. $7000 - 34 =$ _________
30. $3400 - 29 =$ _________

Mental Math 7

Mental Math 8

1.	50 x 5 = __________	16.	800 x 8 = __________
2.	60 x 9 = __________	17.	5 x 60 = __________
3.	500 x 7 = __________	18.	800 x 3 = __________
4.	700 x 8 = __________	19.	8 x 9 = __________
5.	80 x 6 = __________	20.	7 x 70 = __________
6.	9 x 90 = __________	21.	80 x 5 = __________
7.	600 x 6 = __________	22.	600 x 7 = __________
8.	3 x 600 = __________	23.	9 x 70 = __________
9.	40 x 8 = __________	24.	400 x 6 = __________
10.	9 x 500 = __________	25.	900 x 2 = __________
11.	300 x 7 = __________	26.	70 x 4 = __________
12.	3 x 30 = __________	27.	4 x 90 = __________
13.	300 x 9 = __________	28.	400 x 4 = __________
14.	2 x 500 = __________	29.	4 x 200 = __________
15.	30 x 4 = __________	30.	20 x 8 = __________

Mental Math 9

1.	$720 \div 9 =$ ________	16.	$2400 \div 3 =$ ________
2.	$120 \div 6 =$ ________	17.	$490 \div 7 =$ ________
3.	$6300 \div 9 =$ ________	18.	$270 \div 9 =$ ________
4.	$5600 \div 8 =$ ________	19.	$3200 \div 8 =$ ________
5.	$420 \div 7 =$ ________	20.	$180 \div 2 =$ ________
6.	$8100 \div 9 =$ ________	21.	$200 \div 5 =$ ________
7.	$4800 \div 8 =$ ________	22.	$5400 \div 9 =$ ________
8.	$240 \div 6 =$ ________	23.	$1800 \div 3 =$ ________
9.	$450 \div 9 =$ ________	24.	$400 \div 8 =$ ________
10.	$3600 \div 6 =$ ________	25.	$3500 \div 7 =$ ________
11.	$280 \div 4 =$ ________	26.	$360 \div 4 =$ ________
12.	$900 \div 3 =$ ________	27.	$3000 \div 6 =$ ________
13.	$54 \div 9 =$ ________	28.	$210 \div 7 =$ ________
14.	$250 \div 5 =$ ________	29.	$1500 \div 5 =$ ________
15.	$1000 \div 5 =$ ________	30.	$160 \div 4 =$ ________

Mental Math 10

1. $30 \times 8 =$ _________

2. $49 + 71 =$ _________

3. $32 + 47 =$ _________

4. $623 - 88 =$ _________

5. $123 - 7 =$ _________

6. $49 + 17 =$ _________

7. $420 \div 7 =$ _________

8. $82 - 39 =$ _________

9. $300 \div 5 =$ _________

10. $74 - 6 =$ _________

11. $1000 - 330 =$ _________

12. $2 \times 4000 =$ _________

13. $4000 - 62 =$ _________

14. $57 - 32 =$ _________

15. $1111 - 9 =$ _________

16. $145 + 97 =$ _________

17. $2000 - 340 =$ _________

18. $349 + 5 =$ _________

19. $67 + 56 =$ _________

20. $6 \times 500 =$ _________

21. $7 \times 70 =$ _________

22. $29 + 97 =$ _________

23. $1000 - 293 =$ _________

24. $4000 \div 8 =$ _________

25. $8100 - 9 =$ _________

26. $42 + 8 =$ _________

27. $8100 - 90 =$ _________

28. $182 - 95 =$ _________

29. $100 - 62 =$ _________

30. $8100 \div 9 =$ _________

Mental Math 11

1. 12 x 5
    10 x 5   2 x 5
              = 50 + 10

              = _______

2. 12 x 2 = 20 + 4

              = _______

3. 12 x 9 = 90 + 18

              = _______

4. 12 x 4 = _________

5. 12 x 6 = _________

6. 3 x 12 = _________

7. 7 x 12 = _________

8. 8 x 12 = _________

9. 10 x 12 = _________

10. 9 x 12 = _________

11. 11 x 12 = _________

12. 12 x 12 = _________

13. 62 x 3
    60 x 3   2 x 3
              = 180 + 6

              = _______

14. 27 x 3 = 60 + 21

              = _______

15. 12 x 3 = _________

16. 83 x 3 = _________

17. 79 x 3 = _________

18. 44 x 3 = _________

19. 63 x 3 = _________

20. 48 x 3 = _________

21. 58 x 3 = _________

22. 76 x 3 = _________

23. 59 x 3 = _________

24. 73 x 3 = _________

25. 101 x 3 = _________

Mental Math 12

1. $16 \times 5 = 50 + 30$

        $= \underline{\hspace{2cm}}$

2. $16 \times 2 = \underline{\hspace{2cm}}$

3. $16 \times 3 = \underline{\hspace{2cm}}$

4. $16 \times 4 = \underline{\hspace{2cm}}$

5. $16 \times 1 = \underline{\hspace{2cm}}$

6. $16 \times 7 = \underline{\hspace{2cm}}$

7. $16 \times 3 = \underline{\hspace{2cm}}$

8. $16 \times 8 = \underline{\hspace{2cm}}$

9. $16 \times 7 = \underline{\hspace{2cm}}$

10. $16 \times 9 = \underline{\hspace{2cm}}$

11. $12 \times 9 = \underline{\hspace{2cm}}$

12. $12 \times 4 = \underline{\hspace{2cm}}$

13. $12 \times 8 = \underline{\hspace{2cm}}$

14. $12 \times 7 = \underline{\hspace{2cm}}$

15. $92 \times 3 = \underline{\hspace{2cm}}$

16. $48 \times 3 = \underline{\hspace{2cm}}$

17. $25 \times 2 = \underline{\hspace{2cm}}$

18. $25 \times 3 = \underline{\hspace{2cm}}$

19. $25 \times 4 = \underline{\hspace{2cm}}$

20. $90 \times 6 = \underline{\hspace{2cm}}$

21. $92 \times 6 = \underline{\hspace{2cm}}$

22. $67 \times 5 = \underline{\hspace{2cm}}$

23. $42 \times 8 = \underline{\hspace{2cm}}$

24. $45 \times 4 = \underline{\hspace{2cm}}$

25. $33 \times 7 = \underline{\hspace{2cm}}$

26. $29 \times 9 = \underline{\hspace{2cm}}$

27. $62 \times 3 = \underline{\hspace{2cm}}$

28. $96 \times 4 = \underline{\hspace{2cm}}$

29. $18 \times 8 = \underline{\hspace{2cm}}$

Mental Math 13

1. 4 qt = _______ pt

2. 9 gal = _______ qt

3. 2 pt = _______ c

4. 5 ℓ = _______ ml

5. 6 km = _______ m

6. 1 gal = _______ pt

7. 2 lb = _______ oz

8. 3 ft = _______ in.

9. 8 yd = _______ ft

10. 2 qt = _______ c

11. 4 kg = _______ g

12. 1 m = _______ cm

13. 8 km = _______ m

14. 6 ℓ = _______ ml

15. 7 m = _______ cm

16. 3 km = _______ m

17. 9 yd = _______ ft

18. 5 qt = _______ c

19. 6 m = _______ cm

20. 1 lb = _______ oz

21. 3 kg = _______ g

22. 2 ft = _______ in.

23. 4 ℓ = _______ ml

24. 10 lb = _______ oz

25. 5 gal = _______ pt

26. 6 yd = _______ ft

27. 8 kg = _______ g

28. 7 m = _______ cm

29. 2 gal = _______ c

30. 7 ft = _______ in.

Mental Math 14

1. 60 – 30 = _______

2. 60 – 15 = _______

3. 60 – 45 = _______

4. 60 – 35 = _______

5. 60 – 50 = _______

6. 60 – 25 = _______

7. 60 – 10 = _______

8. 60 – 40 = _______

9. 60 – 20 = _______

10. 60 – 42 = _______

11. 60 – 8 = _______

12. 60 – 27 = _______

13. 60 – 58 = _______

14. 60 – 16 = _______

15. 60 – 33 = _______

Give 12 hour time in 24 hour time: 3:00 p.m. = 15:00

16. 6:00 p.m. = _________

17. 10:00 p.m. = ________

18. 2:30 p.m. = ________

19. 5:15 p.m. = ________

20. 11:20 p.m. = ________

21. 1:12 p.m. = ________

22. 4:05 p.m. = ________

Give 24 hour time in 12 hour time: 15:00 = 3:00 p.m.

23. 16:00 = _________ p.m.

24. 18:00 = _________ p.m.

25. 13:30 = _________ p.m.

26. 19:45 = _________ p.m.

27. 14:08 = _________ p.m.

28. 21:43 = _________ p.m.

Mental Math 15

1.	8 min = _____ seconds	16.	84 months = _____ years
2.	5 years = _____ months	17.	14 days = _____ weeks
3.	7 min = _____ seconds	18.	5 min = _____ seconds
4.	36 months = _____ years	19.	9 weeks = _____ days
5.	140 days = _____ weeks	20.	7 weeks = _____ days
6.	10 years = _____ months	21.	60 months = _____ years
7.	6 hours = _____ minutes	22.	42 days = _____ weeks
8.	49 days = _____ weeks	23.	4 years = _____ months
9.	96 months = _____ years	24.	21 days = _____ weeks
10.	2 years = _____ months	25.	4 hours = _____ minutes
11.	4 weeks = _____ days	26.	72 months = _____ years
12.	3 hours = _____ minutes	27.	3 years = _____ months
13.	9 min = _____ seconds	28.	56 days = _____ weeks
14.	48 months = _____ years	29.	5 weeks = _____ days
15.	35 days = _____ weeks	30.	9 years = _____ months

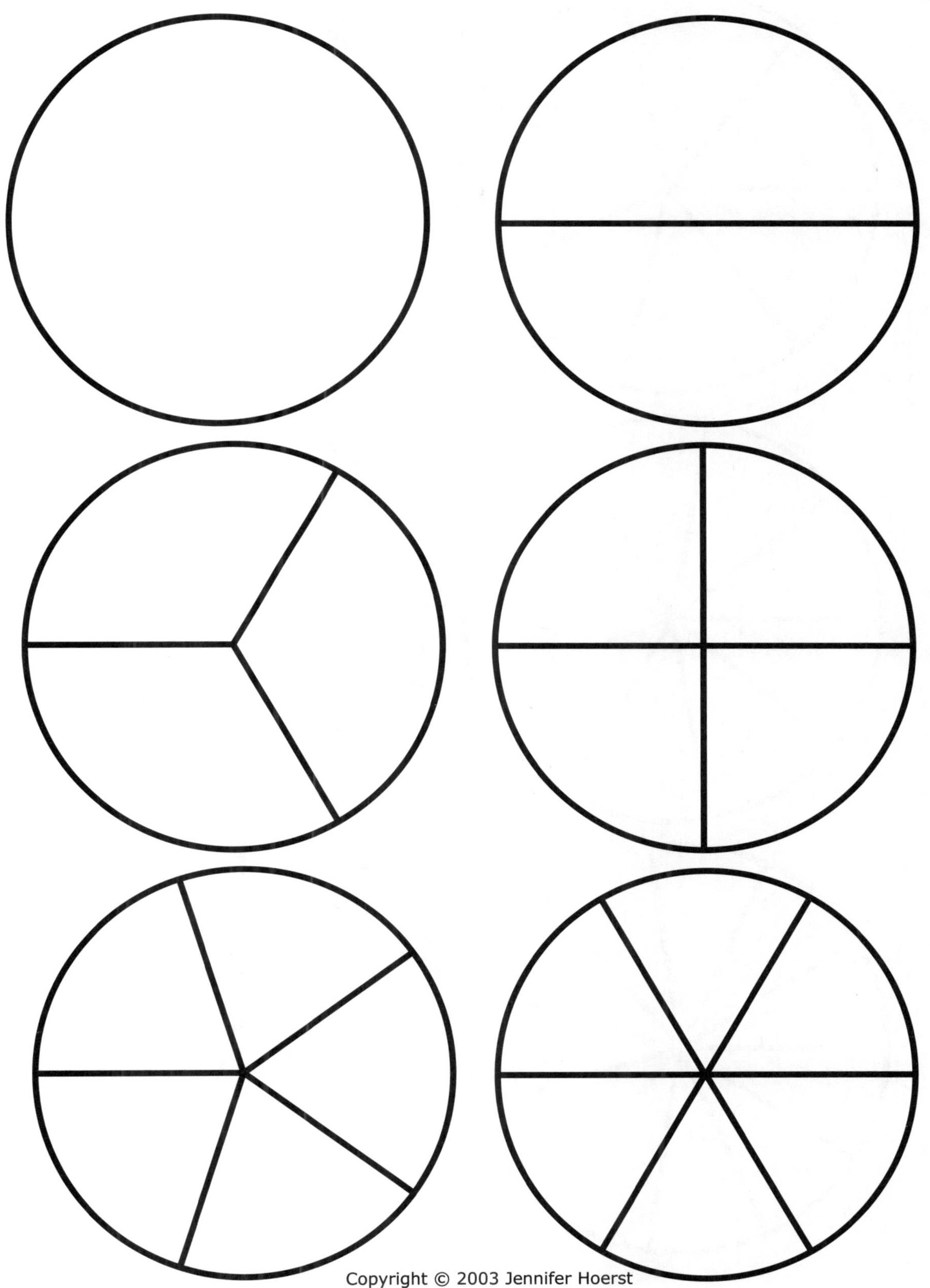

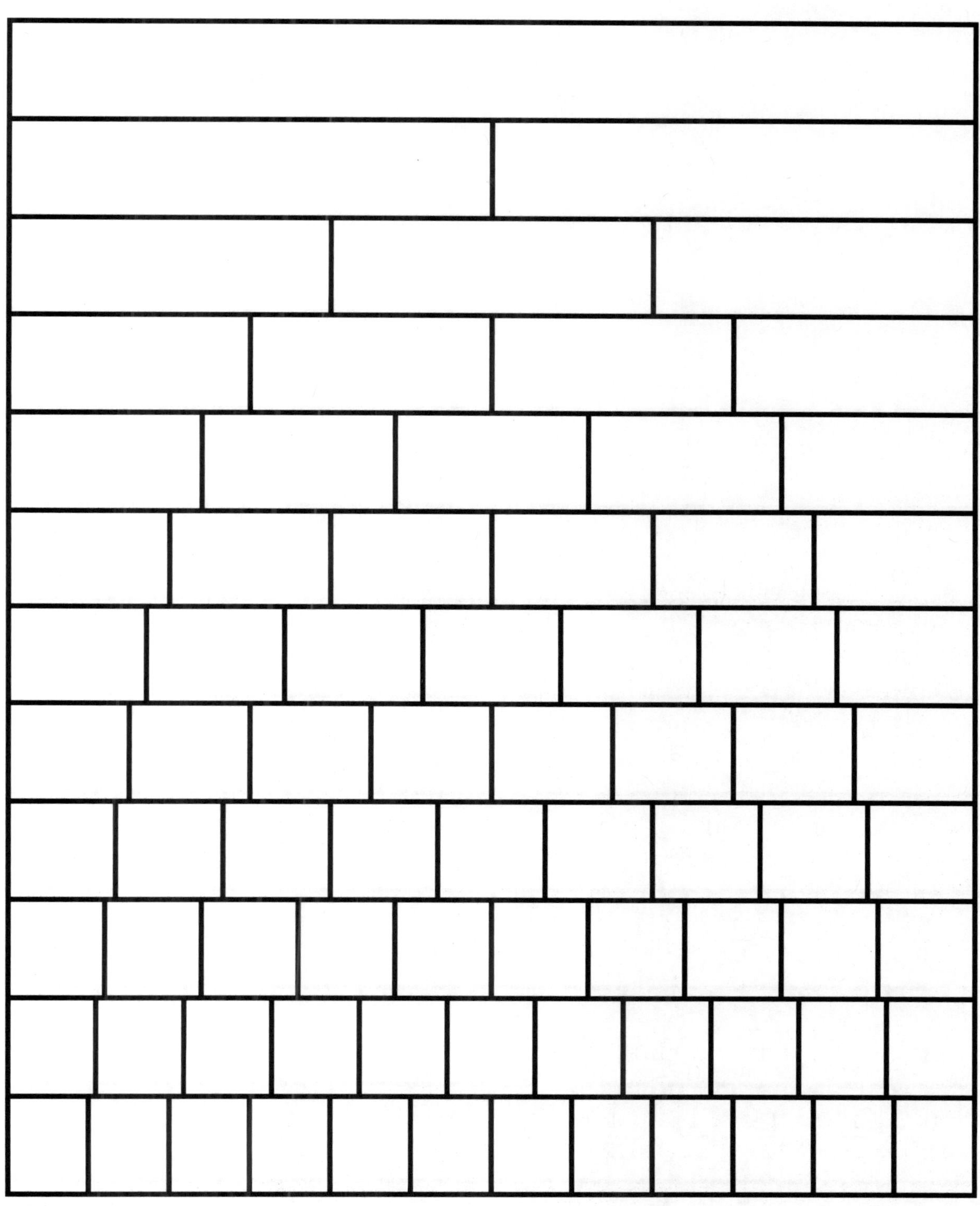

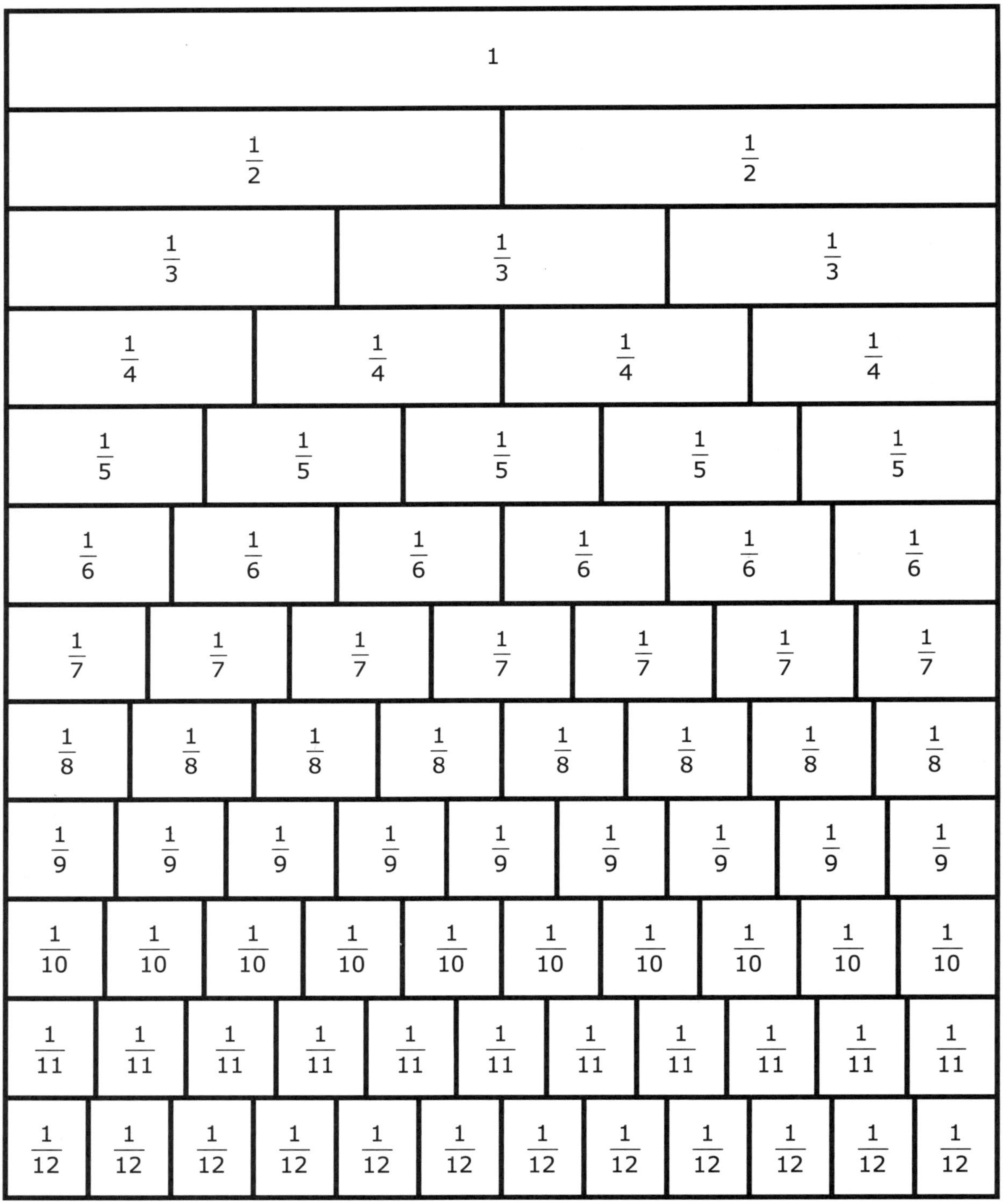

1											
1/2						1/2					
1/3				1/3				1/3			
1/4			1/4			1/4			1/4		
1/5		1/5		1/5		1/5		1/5			
1/6		1/6		1/6	1/6		1/6		1/6		
1/7	1/7		1/7	1/7		1/7	1/7		1/7		
1/8	1/8	1/8	1/8	1/8	1/8	1/8	1/8				
1/9	1/9	1/9	1/9	1/9	1/9	1/9	1/9	1/9			
1/10	1/10	1/10	1/10	1/10	1/10	1/10	1/10	1/10	1/10		
1/11	1/11	1/11	1/11	1/11	1/11	1/11	1/11	1/11	1/11	1/11	
1/12	1/12	1/12	1/12	1/12	1/12	1/12	1/12	1/12	1/12	1/12	1/12

Blank page

Yards, Feet, and Inches

1. (a) 7 ft = _________ in.

    (b) 12 yd = _________ ft

2. A shelf is 1 ft 6 in. high.

    (a) 1 ft 6 in. is _________ in. more than one foot.

    (b) 1 ft 6 in. = _________ in.

3. (a) 5 ft 4 in. is _________ in. longer than five feet.

    (b) 5 ft 4 in. = _________ in.

4. (a) 3 yd 2 ft is _________ ft longer than 3 yards

    (b) 3 yd 2 ft = _________ ft

5. A couch is 14 ft long. It is _________ yd _________ ft long.

6. A ribbon is 30 in. long. What is its length in feet? _________

7. A rope is 15 yd 2 ft long. What is its length in feet?

---

1. Amy has two pieces of yarn. The green yarn is 5 ft 8 in. long and the red yarn is 2 ft 10 in. long. Find the total length of the two pieces of yarn.

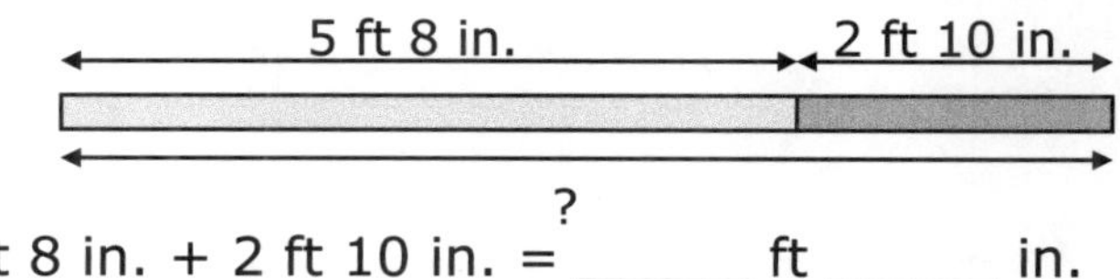

    5 ft 8 in. + 2 ft 10 in. = _________ ft _________ in.

2. Brett had two sticks. The first one was 4 yd 1 ft long and the second one was 2 yd 2 ft long. How much longer is the first one than the second one?

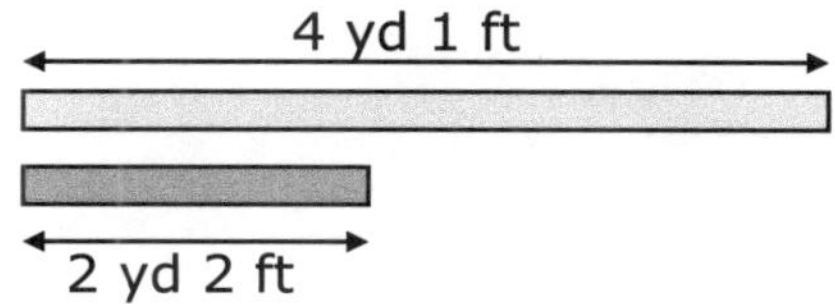

    4 yd 1 ft – 2 yd 2 ft = _________ yd _________ ft

Exercise 10a

1. Write in feet.

   (a)   10 yd 2 ft = _______________ ft

   (b)   6 yd 1 ft = _____________ ft

   (c)   12 yd = ____________ ft

   (d)   150 yd 2 ft = __________ ft

2. Write in inches.

   (a) 3 ft 11 in. = __________ in.

   (b) 9 ft 8 in. = __________ in.

   (c) 10 ft 5 in. = __________ in.

   (d) 7 ft 10 in. = __________ in.

3. Write in feet and inches

   (a) 17 in. = ________ ft _________ in.

   (b) 48 in. = ________ ft _________ in.

   (c) 26 in. = ________ ft _________ in.

4. Write in yards and feet.

   (a) 20 ft = ________ yd _________ ft

   (b) 42 ft = ________ yd _________ ft

   (c) 206 ft = ________ yd _________ ft

   (d) 400 ft = ________ yd _________ ft

5. Put in order from shortest to longest.

    (a) 1 yd 2 ft   4 ft   39 in.   1 m

    (b) 1 ft 10 in.   26 in.   10 cm   2 ft

6. Study the treasure map (X marks the treasure) and answer the questions below.

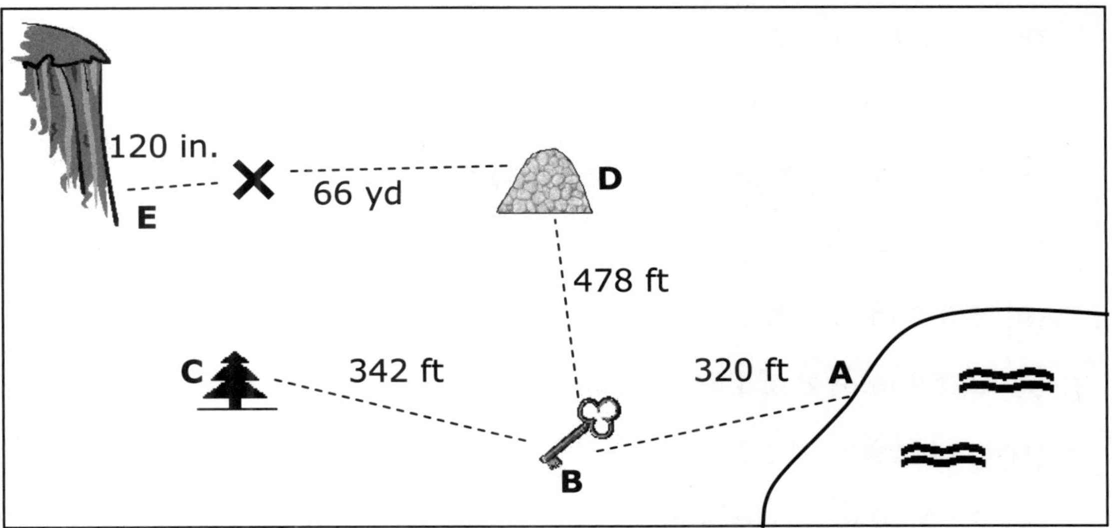

    (a) What is the distance between the shore (A) and the pine tree (C) in yards and feet?

    (b) What is the distance from the key (B) to the treasure in feet?

    (c) How far is the treasure from the foot of the cliff in feet? How far is it in yards and feet?

    (d) A pirate hiked from the shore (A) to the key (B) and then to the rock pile (D) where he was ambushed. Give the distance he hiked in yards and feet.

Exercise 11a

1. Add in compound units

    (a) 2 ft 11 in. + 5 in. = _______ ft _______ in.

    (b) 3 ft 9 in. + 11 in. = _______ ft _______ in.

    (c) 4 ft 7 in. + 8 in. = _______ ft _______ in.

    (d) 5 yd 2 ft + 2 ft = _______ yd _______ ft

    (e) 6 yd 2 ft + 4 yd 2 ft = _______ yd _______ ft

    (f) 8 yd 1 ft + 12 yd 1 ft = _______ yd _______ ft

    (g) 12 yd 2 ft + 18 yd 2 ft = _______ yd _______ ft

    (h) 6 ft 9 in. + 3 ft 9 in. = _______ ft _______ in.

    (i) 3 ft 8 in. + 8 ft 4 in. = _______ ft _______ in.

    (j) 13 ft 11 in. + 6 ft 6 in. = _______ ft _______ in.

    (k) 22 ft 10 in. + 6 ft 5 in. = _______ ft _______ in.

    (l) 140 ft 2 in. + 235 ft 6 in. = _______ ft _______ in.

2. Subtract in compound units

    (a) 3 ft 8 in. − 6 in. = _______ ft _______ in.

    (b) 6 ft 4 in. − 7 in. = _______ ft _______ in.

    (c) 10 ft 5 in. − 6 in. = _______ ft _______ in.

    (d) 6 yd 1 ft − 1 ft = _______ yd _______ ft

    (e) 8 yd 1 ft − 2 ft = _______ yd _______ ft

    (f) 7 yd 2 ft − 5 yd 1 ft = _______ yd _______ ft

    (g) 13 yd 1 ft − 1 yd 2 ft = _______ yd _______ ft

(h) 18 yd 1 ft – 6 yd 2 ft = _______ yd ________ ft

(i)   7 ft 3 in. – 2 ft 11 in. = _______ ft ________ in.

(j)   12 ft 10 in. – 5 ft 9 in. = _______ ft ________ in.

(k) 17 ft 8 in. – 6 ft 10 in. = _______ ft ________ in.

(l)   33 ft 10 in. – 16 ft 6 in. = _______ ft ________ in.

3. John has a board that is 6 ft 3 in. long. He needs a board that is 30 inches long. How long a piece must he saw off of the board to get the piece 30 inches long? Give your answer in feet and inches.

4. It is 12 ft 4 inches from the back door of a kitchen to an arch between the kitchen and the living room.   It is 24 ft 8 inches from this arch to a window in the living room. How far is it, in yards and feet, from the back door to the window in the living room?

5. It is 1,390 miles from Boston to Minneapolis and 1,650 miles from Minneapolis to Seattle.

(a) How far is it from Boston to Seattle?

(b) How much further is it from Minneapolis to Seattle than from Minneapolis to Boston?

Practice 2D

1. Write in feet or inches.

   (a) 6 yd = _______ ft   (b) 7 ft = _______ in.

   (c) 2 ft 10 in. = _______ in.   (d)   6 ft 7 in. = _______ in.

   (e) 108 yd 1 ft = _______ ft   (f)   43 yd 2 ft = _______ ft

2. Write in compound units.

   (a) 25 ft = _______ yd _______ ft   (b) 204 ft = _______ yd _______ ft

   (c) 314 ft = _______ yd _______ ft   (d) 100 ft = _______ yd _______ ft

   (e) 16 in. = _______ ft _______ in.   (f) 26 in. = _______ ft _______ in.

3. Subtract.

   (a) 1 yd – 2 ft = _______ ft   (b) 1 ft – 8 in. = _______ in.

   (c) 42 ft – 41 ft 5 in. = _______ in.   (d) 1 yd – 2 ft 6 in. = _______ in.

4. Add or subtract.

   (a) 12 ft 9 in. – 10 ft 11 in. = _______ ft _______ in.

   (b) 15 yd 1 ft + 2 ft = _______ yd _______ ft

   (c) 14 yd 1 ft – 3 yd 2 ft = _______ yd _______ ft

   (d) 12 yd 2 ft – 5 yd = _______ yd _______ ft

   (e) 15 ft 1 in. – 6 ft 2 in. = _______ ft _______ in.

   (f) 344 ft 11 in. + 132 ft 6 in. = _______ ft _______ in.

5. Put >, <, or = in the circles.

   (a) 1 mile ◯ 5820 feet   (b) 1 inch ◯ 1 centimeter

   (c) 1 yard ◯ 1 meter   (d) 1 yard ◯ 36 inches

Pounds and Ounces

1.   1 lb = 16 oz

(a) 4 lb = _________ oz

(b) 4 lb 4 oz = _________ oz more than 4 lb

(c) 4 lb 4 oz = _________ oz

2. (a) 32 oz = _______ lb

(b) 35 oz = _______ lb _________ oz

3. (a) 10 lb + 14 oz = _________ lb _________ oz

(b) 10 lb 3 oz + 14 oz = _________ lb _________ oz

(c) 10 lb 3 oz + 3 lb 14 oz = _________ lb _________ oz

4. (a) 1 lb − 6 oz = _______ oz

(b) 5 lb 5 oz − 5 oz = _________ lb _______ oz

(c) 5 lb 5 oz − 6 oz = _________ lb _______ oz

(d) 5 lb 5 oz − 1 lb 6 oz = _______ lb _________ oz

5. (a) A pumpkin weighs 8 lb 6 oz. Write the weight in ounces.

(b) A sack of potatoes weighs 160 oz. Write the weight in pounds.

(c) How much heavier is the sack of potatoes than the pumpkin?

(d) A banana squash weighs 6 lb 14 oz. What is the total weight of the pumpkin and the squash?

6. A can of soup weighs 15 oz. What the total weight of 2 cans of soup in pounds and ounces?

Exercise 16a

1. (a) 8 lb – 6 oz = _________ lb _________ oz

   (b) 3 lb – 8 oz = _________ lb _________ oz

2. Fill in the blanks.

   (a) 3 lb = _________ oz   (b) 6 lb 6 oz = _________ oz

   (c) 8 lb 10 oz = _________ oz   (d) 5 lb 2 oz = _________ oz

   (e) 18 oz = _____ lb _____ oz   (f) 32 oz = _____ lb _____ oz

3. Put in order from lightest to heaviest

   (a)   21 oz   1 gram   1 kilogram   1 lb 7 oz

4. Add or subtract in compound units.

   (a) 6 lb 12 oz + 7 lb 5 oz = _________ lb _________ oz

   (b) 12 lb 12 oz + 7 lb 4 oz = _________ lb _________ oz

   (c) 33 lb 8 oz + 22 lb 11 oz = _________ lb _________ oz

   (d) 10 lb 4 oz – 3 lb 15 oz = _________ lb _________ oz

   (e) 40 lb – 18 lb 2 oz = _________ lb _________ oz

   (f) 100 lb – 98 lb 12 oz = _________ lb _________ oz

5. The total weight of two watermelons is 20 lb. The larger watermelon weighs 13 lb 9 oz. What is the weight of the smaller watermelon?

6. An apple weighs 4 oz. Some bananas weigh 10 oz more than the apple. A bunch of grapes weighs three times as much as the bananas. What is the weight of the grapes?

Practice 3D

1. Fill in the blanks.

    (a) 10 lb = __________ oz

    (b) 7 lb 15 oz = ________ oz

    (c) 9 lb 9 oz = __________ oz

    (d) 24 oz = ________ lb __________ oz

    (e) 33 oz = ________ lb ________ oz

2. Add or subtract in compound units.

    (a)   10 lb 7 oz + 13 oz = ________ lb ________ oz

    (b)   4 lb 11 oz + 6 lb 11 oz = ________ lb________ oz

    (c)   18 lb – 12 lb 3 oz = ________ lb________ oz

    (d)   15 lb 12 oz – 3 lb 5 oz = ________ lb________ oz

3. One squash weighs 4 lb 8 oz. Another squash weighs 2 lb 10 oz.
    (a) What is the total weight of the two squashes?

    (b) What is the difference in weight between the two squashes?

4. Two packages of cheese and a box of crackers together weigh 3 lb. The
    box of crackers alone weighs 1 lb 12 oz.

    (a) How much does one package of cheese weigh?

    (b) If Mary paid $2 for the two packages of cheese, what is the cost of
         1 oz of cheese?

Gallons, Quarts, Pints, and Cups

1. A carton of half-and-half holds 1 pint. How many cups is this?

2. A carton of milk holds 1 quart. How many pints is this? How many cups?

3. The capacity of a milk jug is 1 gallon. It is also 4 quarts. What is the capacity of the jug in cups?

4. (a) 1 gal 3 qt is _______ qt more than 1 gal

    (b) 1 gal 3 qt = _______ qt

5. (a) 1 qt = _______ pt

    (b) 4 pt = _______ c

    (b) 8 c = _______ qt

    (c) 10 c = _______ qt _______ pt

6. There are 5 cartons of milk. Each carton contains 1 qt of milk.

    (a) The total amount of milk in the five cartons is _______ gal _______ qt.

    (b) The total amount of milk in the five cartons is _______ c.

Exercise 23a

1. Put >, <, or = in the circles.

    (a) 3 pt ◯ 7 c   (b) 8 pt 1 c ◯ 18 c

    (c) 33 c ◯ 2 gal   (d) 30 qt ◯ 7 gal 2 qt

2. Put in order from smallest amount to largest amount

    4 pt 1 c   20 c   1 gal 2 c   1 liter

3. Add or subtract in compound units

    (a) 12 pt 1 c + 6 pt 1 c = _______ pt ________ c

    (b) 12 gal 3 qt + 9 gal 3 qt = _______ gal _______ qt

    (c) 10 gal 1 qt − 8 gal 3 qt = _______ gal _______ qt

    (d) 36 qt − 15 qt 3 c = _______ qt _______ c

4. One fish tank has a capacity of 15 gal 2 qt.
    The second fish tank has a capacity of 14 gal 3 qt.

    (a) What is the total capacity of the two fish tanks?

    (b) What is the difference in capacity of the two fish tanks?

Practice 4D

1. Fill in the blanks.

   (a)   10 pt = _________ c   (b) 8 pt 1 c = _________ c

   (c)   7 qt = _______ pt   (d) 12 qt 1 pt = _______ pt

   (e)   12 gal = _______ qt   (f) 5 gal 2 qt = _______ qt

2. Fill in the circle with >, =, or <

   (a) 5 gal 2 qt ◯ 23 qt

   (b) 22 qt 1 pt ◯ 40 pt

   (c) 6 qt 1 c ◯ 25 c

3. Add or subtract.

   (a)   10 qt 1 pt + 3 qt 1 pt = _______ qt _______ pt

   (b)   100 gal 4 qt − 14 gal 1 qt = _______gal _______ qt

   (c)   301 pt − 276 pt 1 c = _______ pt _______ c

4. Mr. Jones bought 6 gallons of milk for his 4 teenage boys. They drank 3 gal 1 qt in 3 days. How much milk was left?

5. Devon drinks 2 cups of milk daily. How many quarts of milk does he drink in 2 weeks?

6. The capacity of a jug is 1 gal. There is one pint of water in it now. How many more pints of water are needed to fill it up?

7.   The capacity of a tank is 84 qt. How many gallons of water can it hold?